R THE MILLENNIUM

André Breton: Selections. Edited and with an Introduction by Mark Polizzotti

María Sabina: Selections. Edited by Jerome Rothenberg, with Texts and Commentaries by Álvaro Estrada and Others

The publisher gratefully acknowledges the generous contribution to this book provided by the General Endowment Fund of the Associates of the University of California Press.

MARÍA SABINA: SELECTIONS

SELECTIONS

MARÍA SABINA

EDITED BY JEROME ROTHENBERG

With Texts and Commentaries

by Álvaro Estrada and Others

UNIVERSITY OF CALIFORNIA PRESS

Berkeley Los Angeles London

University of California Press
Berkeley and Los Angeles, California

University of California Press, Ltd.
London, England

© 2003 by the Regents of the University of California

Library of Congress Cataloging-in-Publication Data
María Sabina, 1894–
María Sabina : Selections / María Sabina ; edited by Jerome Rothenberg ;
with texts and commentaries by Álvaro Estrada and others.
p. cm. — (Poets for the millennium ; 2)
Includes bibliographical references.
ISBN 0-520-23360-3 (cloth : alk. paper) —
ISBN 0-520-23953-9 (pbk : alk. paper)
1. María Sabina, 1894–. 2. Mazatec Indians—Biography.
3. Mazatec poetry. 4. Mazatec Indians—Medicine. 5. Mazatec Indians—
Rites and ceremonies. 6. Mushrooms, Hallucinogenic—Mexico.
I. Rothenberg, Jerome, 1931–. II. Titles. III. Series.
F1121.M35M3772 2003
299ʹ.786—dc21 [B] 2003042605

Manufactured in the United States of America
10 09 08 07 06 05 04 03
10 9 8 7 6 5 4 3 2 1

CONTENTS

In Mazatec, María Sabina's calling was, literally, that of "wise woman" —a term that we may choose to translate as "shaman" or, by a further twist, as "poet." But that's to bring it and her into our own generalized kind of reckoning and naming. In much the same way, the book containing her oral autobiography, or *vida,* which first appeared in Spanish in 1977 and which makes up a large part of the present volume, translated her from the particularities of local Mazatec culture to the generalities of a book and media technology that can travel almost anywhere. (Or so we like to think.)

When I visited Mexico in the summer of 1979 to arrange for publication and translation of her *Vida* into English, the film *María Sabina: Mujer Espíritu,* a documentary by Nicolás Echevarría, was playing under government sponsorship at the large Cine Régis in downtown Mexico City. María Sabina herself had been brought to Mexico City the previous month—a small, elderly Indian woman, dressed in the traditional bird and flower huipil, and with only a touch of Spanish at her service—and had been much patronized (even lionized, I think the word is) before her return to her native Huautla, a small and remote hill town in the mountains of Oaxaca. (All this in contrast to the attempt, a dozen years before, to arrest her for practice of the sacred mushroom ceremonies that existed in the Mazatecan sierras long before the first conquerors set foot there.)

I hope, in calling attention to the degree of fame she has, that I don't frustrate the reader's enthusiasm for things Indian and remote. She was certainly aware of being famous ("the judge knows me, the government knows me," she sings), though by our standards it had little effect on her life per se. She continued to live in her old tin-roofed house—even while a new prefabricated home supplied by the government was going up nearby. She continued to walk barefoot up the hillside, to speak Mazatec, not Spanish, to cure and to shamanize, to smoke cigarettes and drink beer from the bottle, to celebrate her own life of labor and her ability to make a clean bed, along with those other powers, language foremost among them, that had won her local and international repute. A poet, in short, with a sense of both a real physical world and a world beyond what the mind may sense, or the mouth proclaim.

Before her name reached us clearly, her image and words had already come into our world. By the late 1950s, R. Gordon Wasson's recording, *The Mushroom Ceremony of the Mazatec Indians of Mexico,* was in circulation, and even before, *Life* magazine had run a feature (part of a "Great Adventures Series") on Wasson's "discovery of mushrooms that cause strange visions."[1] Soon thereafter one heard from travelers in Mexico of side trips to see and be illumined by the "mushroom woman" of Oaxaca. (Her own view of these matters awaits the reader, within.) And in the strange way in which ideas about language may travel in advance of the language itself, the Spanish Nobel poet Camilo José Cela constructed, early along, a highly fantastical opera about her, *María Sabina y el carro de heno, o el inventor de la guillotina*—a takeoff in part on what he took, from what was

1. May 13, 1957. The cover, which mentions the Wasson piece as one of its headlines, also shows a photo of comedian Bert Lahr ("as a bumbling lover") peering through tropical fronds—a curious example, so to speak, of cultural synchronism.

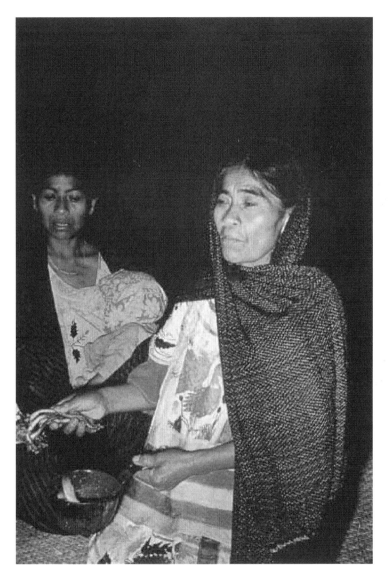

María Sabina incensing the mushrooms. *Photograph by Allan Richardson.*
Courtesy R. Gordon Wasson Archives, Harvard University, Cambridge, Massachusetts.

then available, to be her style of languaging.[2] In Mexico she became the subject of at least one comic book and of other forms of popular diffusion, and the American poet Anne Waldman, having come across the liner notes to Wasson's *Ceremony,* circa 1970, used them to model a work called *Fast Speaking Woman* that she performed in poetry readings and even, if memory doesn't fail me, as part of Bob Dylan's short-lived Rolling Thunder Review or of his film *Renaldo and Clara:*

> I'm a shouting woman
> I'm a speech woman
> I'm an atmosphere woman
> I'm an airtight woman

in distinct reflection of the other's:

> I am a spirit woman, says
> I am a lord eagle woman, says

—which the North American poet acknowledges formally as her "indebtedness to the Mazatec Indian Shamaness in Mexico." Yet she fails at that point to name her—with a sense, one guesses, that the "shamaness" is of the anonymous tribal/oral sort. But María Sabina was already in "the world" by then—beyond the boundaries of her own place, to be given a measure of fame and the Western trappings of immortality-through-written-language that she herself could hardly have sought.

The confusion, as such, is easy enough to understand. María Sabina is Mazatec without question, and the mode of her chants (the way the

2. "I'm a woman who cries / I'm a woman who spits / I'm a woman who pisses / I'm a woman who gives milk no longer / I'm a woman who speaks / I'm a woman who shouts / I'm a woman who vomits / I'm an unrefined woman but I know how to fight against death and the grass that brought forth its venom" (C. J. Cela).

words go, etc.) is not merely personal but common to other Mazatec shamans. Among them she stands out—not alone but sharing a language with the other great ones, including those "tiger shamans" we hear of in the hills, who rarely make themselves visible in the town environs of Huautla.

This book, then, is centrally hers.

But it is as well a book of transmissions, of which Waldman's (like my own) is a curious and distant instance. The songs, the words, come to María Sabina through the agency of what Henry Munn has elsewhere called "the mushrooms of language." (Her qualification of each line with the word *tso,* "says," is a testimony to that: that it is not María Sabina but the unspoken he/she/it whose words these are.) Then, sometime past the middle of her life, R. Gordon Wasson begins the other transmission that carries her words over great distances: an offshoot of his studies of mushroom history and lore but one that continued to affect him for the rest of his life.

The transmission most crucial to this book is that between María Sabina and Álvaro Estrada. A Mazatec speaker and fellow townsman, Estrada engaged her in a series of recorded conversations, which he translated into Spanish and made the basis of her "oral autobiography." To this he added a new translation of Wasson's 1956 recording and a series of footnotes and commentaries, not as an outside observer but with a native feel for Mazatec particulars and with testimony from older members of his own family and from other Mazatecs, local shamans among them, still deeply involved in the native religion. He is in that sense no innocent Carlos Castaneda nor is María Sabina a shadowy Don Juan, but both stand open before us. The poetry and the vision are nonetheless intense.

On the basis of Estrada's work, I was able to arrange for the publication, in 1981, of *María Sabina: Her Life and Chants.* That book was

Álvaro Estrada and María Sabina. *Photo courtesy of Álvaro Estrada.*

part of an unrealized series of books, New Wilderness Poetics, that I
had intended as a bringing together of ethnopoetic and experimental
poetries under the imprint of Ross-Erikson Publishers in Santa Bar-
bara, California. With the death of publisher Buzz Erikson and the
suspension of the press, the book, while published, had only a very
limited circulation.

In the Ross-Erikson version, the active translator and commenta-
tor was Henry Munn, who was also my own contact to María Sabina
and the Mazatec ritual world. Continuing the process begun by
Estrada, Munn added a second chanting session (the sole recorded one
in which only Mazatecs were present), along with additional observa-
tions from both "inside" and "outside" points of view. Munn's con-

nection was itself a part of the recent history of Huautla. His entry there, circa 1965, was as one of those "oddballs"—visitors to Huautla in the 1960s—cited by Wasson in an accompanying "retrospective essay"; but Munn was a genuine seeker as well, and after the "great bust of 1967," he returned to Huautla, married into the Estrada family, and has since become his own witness and a devoted student of Mazatec culture. An early essay of his, "The Mushrooms of Language," is a brilliant introduction to the verbal side of Mazatec shamanism: a first recognition of the shaman's work as an essentially poetic act and, in the Surrealist master André Breton's definition of *poesis* quoted therein, "a sacred action." Munn's translations (drawing on both Mazatec and Spanish) are equally attentive, and his commentaries there and elsewhere direct us to a range of mythopoetic connections (local and universal) informing the Mazatec chants.

The presence, alongside María Sabina, of Estrada, Munn, and Wasson made of this work a multileveled book of testimony—and something more: a book of exiles and losses. This will seem surprising only if one sentimentalizes or primitivizes the Mazatec present, for the present is perennially a time of loss and change. Viewed in this way, Estrada may appear as the acculturated Mazatec, whose adolescence coincided with the arrival in Huautla of anonymous hippies and world-famous superstars in search of God, and who early on withdrew to work in Mexico as a writer and engineer. However, Estrada's yearning here (as it came across to me in conversation with him) is for something that draws him backward, that fascinates and troubles him, and that he cannot possess; he honors it, but mostly he lives apart from it. With Munn, the stance—of exile and escape—seemed different from the start: a flight-from-time in search of mysteries/illuminations that brought him to the place left vacant by Estrada: the town, the family, and so on.

But overshadowing them both is the culturally authentic, strangely marginal figure of María Sabina, whose personal history (never "erased" in the Castanedan sense) is always precarious and whose spiritual universe begins to change (she tells us) with the coming of the blond strangers, a few at first, then in great waves in the 1960s. With a sense of what was at stake and of his own role in the subsequent engulfment of Mazatec culture, Wasson, accused, responded as poignant witness: "[Her] words make me wince. I, Gordon Wasson, am held responsible for the end of a religious practice in Mesoamerica that goes back far, for millennia. 'The little mushrooms won't work anymore. There is no helping it.' I fear she spoke the truth, exemplifying her *sabiduría*." And, still more strikingly, the words of another shaman count the losses for Estrada: "What is terrible, listen, is that the divine mushroom no longer belongs to us. Its sacred language has been profaned. The language has been spoiled and it is indecipherable for us."

The word "language" hits here with tremendous force; for this is crucially a book of language, a reflection of the great Book of Language that María Sabina saw in her initiatory vision:

> On the Principal Ones' table a book appeared, an open book that went on growing until it was the size of a person. In its pages there were letters. It was a white book, so white it was resplendent.
>
> One of the Principal Ones spoke to me and said: "María Sabina, this is the Book of Wisdom. It is the Book of Language. Everything that is written in it is for you. The Book is yours, take it so that you can work." I exclaimed with emotion: "That is for me. I receive it."

And she did and was thereafter a woman of language—what we would dare to translate, by a comparison to those most deeply into it among us, as "poet."

Her own words and her highly tuned chants (the improvised and collaged "sessions" that function like long, driving poems) make this clear. Wasson's account of her actual performance and its impact on the first enthralled outsiders brings the message home, as do the appraisals by poets (Homero Aridjis, Waldman) from outside her time and place. And hearing her voice on tape or reading her here in translation, we catch the presence of a great oral poet, one whom we can now see working and changing over the course of time—in three recorded sessions, 1956, 1958, and 1970. The Language revealed is awesome, not because it allows her to control the world around her (it doesn't) but because it lets her survive the sufferings of a world in which the spirit of Language itself has been "profaned," in which "it wanders without direction in the atmosphere ... not only the divine spirit ... but our own spirit, the spirit of the Mazatecs, as well."

A devastatingly human book and testimony, hers is an appropriate inclusion for a series on millennial poetics over a broad human range. This broadening and expansion was the motive for those of us who entered some years ago into the pursuit of an actual "ethnopoetics"— a term the poet David Antin expanded still further to mean "Human Poetics ... People's Poetics or the poetics of natural language." And other-than-human as well, if we take her word for it: "Language belongs to the saint children"—the sacred mushrooms—"They speak and I have the power to translate." Or Antin further: "What I take the 'poetics' part of ETHNOPOETICS to be is the structure of those linguistic acts of invention and discovery through which the mind explores the transformational power of language and discovers and invents the world and itself."

In that sense we aren't dealing with something merely alien/exotic, but we are all potential witnesses and transmitters, all suffering exiles and losses, all in an encounter with language and vision. María Sabina's Language bears the traces of such an encounter and presents them in a form in no way incomplete: a language-centered poetics and a guide that encompasses even that writing which we would still speak of, in our arrogance, as the final instrument of language that separates her and us. But she has seen the book as well—the Book of Language—and that makes of her own work and Estrada's a Book about the Book. And, if we let it, it is also a book of healing: a language directed against that *sparagmos*—that classic split in consciousness—that tears us all asunder. The wounds are deep and probably irremediable, but the dream, while we're alive, is that of wholeness. Here is language as a medicine, its ancient function; for, as she puts it elsewhere, "with words we live and grow," and (again speaking of the mushrooms with a familiar Mazatec word) "I cured them with the Language of the *children*."

ADDENDUM TO A PRE-FACE

The series of books for which this volume serves as a crucial anchor/ pivot aims to present a range of poets whose work, taken *ensemble,* will give a sense of the changes that have affected our ideas of poetry over the preceding century and the beginnings of the present century and millennium. To bring María Sabina into such an ensemble is to question the boundaries of poetry as a matter of literature, at least in the way in which those words—"poetry" and "literature"—are commonly understood. That questioning, of course, is precisely the point of her inclusion here—an experiment in definition that attempts to see what happens when we place beside the experimental poets of our time one whom Henry Munn calls "a genius [who] emerges from the soil of the communal, religious-therapeutic folk poetry of a native Mexican campesino people." Or going a step further, it is an attempt to explore what the Mexican poet Homero Aridjis means when he speaks of her, unequivocally, as "la más grande poeta visionaria de América Latina en el siglo XX" ("Lo indígena es bello," in *La Reforma,* March 18, 2001), or elsewhere as "one of the best poets, not only of Mexico but of the entire American continent." (See page 164.)

In constructing the present gathering, I have tried to avoid the impression that María Sabina is being presented here as herself a kind of experimentalist. (Henry Munn's new essay, below, makes her traditionalism, however different from our own, abundantly clear.) Nor is she a poet in her own terms but a Wise One and a healer—functions to which some poets of our own (and not the least among them) have aspired in a culture foreign to the values and assumptions of her religion and her shamanism. At the same time it's clear that she was a contemporary of ours in many fundamental ways—supported and abused by the same powers that have impinged on all our lives and works. So a balance has had to be struck between our differences and similarities, even while recognizing that most readers will come to the work with their own presuppositions and that little can be done as editor (also with presuppositions) to counteract them.

The principal intention of this book, then, is to present María Sabina as a poet—more precisely, to present her Language—both as structure and as vision—as a kind of poetry. It is a context in which she has rarely been presented or considered, except by a relatively small number of active contemporary poets. Her works, as written down by others, take up most of the pages that follow; they are the heart of the book, far more intrinsic than the commentaries about them. The first work and the key to all the others is her *Vida*—a construction by Álvaro Estrada based on a long series of disconnected interviews that he carried on with her in the Mazatec language. This leads in turn to a full translation—by Henry Munn and others—of the earliest of her recorded chants (her "poetry" as such), transcribed by Wasson in 1956 and disseminated not long thereafter by Folkways Records. With Wasson's "mushroom velada"[3] recording of 1958 and the 1970 recording (attended only by fellow Mazatecs), this constitutes the body of her surviving work. And because the three chants vary and supplement each other in a number of ways, I have included not only the full Folkways chant but also excerpts from the other two (the "mushroom velada" one in a differently inflected translation by George M. and Florence H. Cowan) as a way of filling out—enriching—the work presented here.

As with the other books in the series, the rest is (largely) commentary—an effort in this case to provide a context for the *Vida* and the Chants, along with a sense of how María Sabina's words and life have affected poets over a wider human range. In a section designated as "Commentaries and Derivations," the opening voice is that of Álvaro Estrada, who provides an introduction both to her *Vida* and to his own seminal role in its composition. The three accounts that follow are from observers who have been close to her: the description by Wasson and his wife, Valentina Pavlovna Wasson, of an early performance session and of their responses to it; a detailed discussion by Henry Munn comparing María Sabina's chants to those of other Mazatec shamans; and Homero Aridjis's description of his interchange with her in the last years of her life.

Aridjis's short essay is the first of several excerpts from contemporary poets who have responded to her as a woman of language, whose work has a meaning outside of its place and moment of origin. At a still greater remove Anne Waldman is represented with both an excerpt from *Fast Speaking Woman* and an essay on how that work de-

3. The Spanish word *velada* ("vigil" or "soirée") was Wasson's choice as the general term for the the the all-night shamanic sessions. It was also, he tells us, customarily used by Spanish-speaking Mazatecs.

veloped from a first sighting of María Sabina's chants and how the chants themselves fit into the framework (North American and Buddhist) of Waldman's poetry and world. My own poem, "The Little Saint of Huautla," is a meditation, more or less, on a 1979 meeting with María Sabina. And the final derivation is, by contrast, that of Juan Gregorio Regino, a younger Mazatec poet writing in the native language and with an awareness of his own relation to—and divergence from—the workings of the older Mazatec shaman-poets: the *chjinie,* as he names them in the work translated below, beginning with some lines by María Sabina. To the extent that poetry and language are communal activities—"made by all and not by one," as the Surrealists once had it—Regino's work brings the *lengua mazateca* that he shares with her into a dynamic, always changing present.

That much I think is understood by all those who have contributed to this book. For me the two key figures here were Munn, who was my personal guide, and Estrada, without whom María Sabina would have remained in the anonymous condition imposed on indigenous peoples by the external dominant cultures. If Estrada is the de facto author of this book, in a sense Munn is the de facto co-editor—a knowledgeable and passionate observer and participant, who for more than thirty years has worked on the intellectual and poetic dimensions of the Mazatec and Mesoamerican experience. I would be remiss not to call attention to his patient and persistent work, and if this book were to have a dedication, it would surely be to him.

Jerome Rothenberg, 1980/2003

THE LIFE *Written with Álvaro Estrada*

I don't know in what year I was born, but my mother, María Concepción, told me that it was in the morning of the day they celebrate the Virgin Magdalene, there in Río Santiago, an *agencia* of the municipality of Huautla. None of my ancestors knew their age.[1]

My mother was born and raised in a place near Huautla on the way to San Andrés Hidalgo. My father, Crisanto Feliciano, was born and raised in Río Santiago. When they started to live together—they didn't get married—she was around fourteen and he twenty. My mother had lived three years with her man when I was born. I was baptized right away. My baptismal godparents were Juan Manuel and María Sebastiana, a campesino couple who felt a lot of affection for my father. My mother gave birth to María Ana, my sister, when I was two years old. We were the only two children born to them. I didn't know my father very well, since he died when I was three years old. I know that he was a very hard worker. He planted maize and beans on land he had succeeded in buying with his work. He sold what he harvested at the market in Huautla or in neighboring towns. Our home in Río Santiago was a little hut with walls of mud plastered over a bamboo

1. On August 25, 1976, the parish priest Arturo García issued a baptismal certificate for María Sabina, based on the original facts recorded in the archive of the Huautla church. One can see that the names of the baptismal godparents registered in the document don't coincide with those given by María Sabina. Nevertheless it should be pointed out that even today it is difficult to know the exact name of some Mazatecs because of their deficient pronunciation of Spanish names.

framework, and a thatched roof of sugarcane leaves. My mother made the tortillas and put the pot of beans, which she later served to each of us, on the fire. With our meals, we drank *pinole* water sweetened with cane sugar. It was drunk hot. At that time there was no coffee; few people grew it. We went to bed before it got dark. My father left to work the land very early, a little after the first rooster crowed. We slept on the ground, on mats, with our clothes on. That's how we all slept.

At the birth of my sister, María Ana, my father was already sick. There was no remedy for his sickness because the origin of his illness wasn't a matter of this world, but a punishment of the powerful Lord of Thunder who takes care of and gives fertility to what is sown. The thing is that my father, when he was still single, had aroused the anger of this great and powerful Lord. The story is as follows:

One dawn the young Crisanto Feliciano started for his field to clear it; it was necessary to get rid of the leaves and bushes on the land. He took his hoe and his machete. Like all the men of his time, he wore white pants and shirt of pure cotton. On festival days he put on a poncho that reached to his knees and was tied with a silk belt at the waist.

For two days Crisanto Feliciano worked on his land to gather together the leaves and weeds and all the garbage that impeded a good planting; then he formed a pile with it all in a place near someone else's field. Finally he set the pile on fire. The sticks, the dry leaves, and the weeds burned easily. It was late afternoon and the end of the day was near. The wind blew strong, the day had been very hot, and one could feel the dryness. But the flames of the pile got lively, and the wind played with them until they got near the neighboring field; so much so that they burned some corn plants. Seeing that, Crisanto rushed to put out the flames burning in the other's cornfield. Not much was burned, but Crisanto knew that to have damaged the field, even though the damage was slight, could cause his death. He knew that all the crops were protected by the Lord of Thunder: if somebody robbed ears of corn he would die. If a donkey ate in a cornfield, it too would die. Where land was protected like that, neither rats, moles, nor birds hurt it. A crop protected by the Lord of Thunder grows pretty and abundant. Crisanto was condemned to death: he had burned a sacred cornfield. Only some plants, but it was enough to receive the curse of the Lord of Thunder. People who deliberately or imprudently harm a sacred crop suffer from lumps that come out on the chest and neck. The lumps burst when they've matured and turn into purulent and repugnant pimples. Then the people die. The damage that is done to a sacred crop can't be paid for with anything: neither by replacing the destroyed plants, nor by paying the damage in money to the owner.

Crisanto knew that he was lost but he had one hope. His grandfather and his father were Wise Ones:[2] they used *saint children*[3] to speak with the Lords of the Mountains. The Wise Ones can speak with the beings who are the masters of all the things in the world. And they could speak with the Lord of Thunder. They could ask him to pardon

---

2. This term is used frequently in the text. It is the name that is given to the Mazatec shaman. The native words are *chota chjine* (wise person). Among the Mazatecs are found three categories of curers. On the lowest level is the Sorcerer (*tji?e*), who is said to be able to transform himself into an animal (*nagual*) at night. He has a great capacity for doing evil and for turning other people into *naguales*. On the intermediate level is the Curer (*chotaxi v?e'nta*), properly speaking, who uses massage, potions, and devices such as his own language in which he invokes the Lords of different places, mountains, and springs. These two categories are well known in rural Mexico, but in Huautla there is a third and still superior one: that of Wise One and doctor (*chota chjine*), who doesn't do evil or use potions to cure. His therapy— or hers—involves the ingestion of the mushroom, through which he acquires the power to diagnose and cure the sick person, whom he also gives several pairs of mushrooms to eat. [The phonetic symbol ? indicates a glottal stop.]
3. "Saint children," "Little-One-Who-Springs-Forth," "little saints," and "little things" are four euphemistic terms for the mushrooms in Mazatec. María Sabina generally calls them *saint children* or simply *children*.

Crisanto who from imprudence had burned the plants of a protected cornfield.

So thought Crisanto and that gave him hope for his life. Meanwhile he didn't want to alarm his family. He preferred for the moment to keep quiet about his pain. "Later I'll tell them ..." he said to himself.

Months passed and young Crisanto went on hiding his pain.

But on a certain occasion, his father, Pedro Feliciano, stayed awake to eat the *saint children*. There, during the night, the Wise One saw that his son would soon die from the pimples. The following morning, he said: "Crisanto, my son, I've had a terrible vision. I've seen you turned into a turkey. The *Little-One-Who-Springs-Forth* has revealed to me that you are condemned to die. I know the reason as well, the *Little-One-Who-Springs-Forth* himself has told me ..."

In that way, Crisanto found himself obliged to tell his father about the burned cornfield.

His father consoled him, saying: "We will fight against the force of the Lord of Thunder. We will stay awake with *Little-One-Who-Springs-Forth*. We will ask the Lords that you be pardoned." Later the Wise Man, Pedro Feliciano, accompanied by his father, Juan Feliciano, stayed awake several times with the *saint children,* but they didn't obtain anything. They also called in Sorcerers and Sucking Doctors without achieving anything.

Later, one night, as Crisanto tried to sleep, he passed a hand over his chest, and his fingers stopped at the feel of little bumps above his nipples. "What can that be?" he asked himself. With a shock, he realized everything: they were the lumps from the curse that were beginning to break out. He felt fear and deep worry. That night he thought about his life. He thought that he was very young (he would have been around twenty years old), and worry didn't let him sleep for the rest of the night.

The following morning, Crisanto said decisively to his father: "I desire a woman for myself. I've seen a girl on the way to Huautla. She lives with her parents just beyond San Andrés. You could ask for her to come and live with me."

With time the parents asked for the girl, and one day Crisanto went for his woman, María Concepción. He took her to live in Río Santiago.

My father suffered from his illness and my mother understood him. The first lumps burst, forming purulent pimples that later covered his neck and part of his chest.

With the passing years, my father got worse. When I was around three years old, I imagine, and my sister, María Ana, barely four or five months old, he died. Neither the Sorcerers nor the Curers nor the Wise Ones could heal him. Poor man, he died, turned into a turkey. Because the mortal curse of the Lord of Thunder makes one sick little by little. The cursed person lasts years suffering: it can be four, five, six, or seven, in which time the lumps turn into purulent pimples. Some persons condemned to suffer like that resign themselves to die, others fight against the curse of the Lord of Thunder. The Sorcerers speak to where the echo is, to the mountains and the slopes. There they ask for help from the Lord of the Holy Mountain. But little can be done against the curse of the Lord of Thunder. The neck of the sick person looks like that of a turkey. Exactly like that of a turkey. And that is because the Lord of Thunder has at his service a sacred turkey. This turkey is the one who is charged with punishing the persons and animals who dare to damage the crops. The turkey turns the people or animals into turkeys. That's why they die with pimples on their neck. The Sorcerers sacrifice hens, they give money (cacao beans) and turkey eggs to Chicon Nindó.

2

My mother, upon being left a widow, seeing that there was nothing to hope for from her in-laws, decided to return to her parents. She had lived with Crisanto Feliciano for six years. At that time she was still young, somewhere around twenty. My father must have died at twenty-five or twenty-six; I don't know the exact age at which he died.

My maternal grandparents were very poor. My mother brought us to live with them and forgot Río Santiago completely.

My grandfather, Manuel Cosme, already quite an old man, worked as a peon for the landholders. My grandmother, María Estefanía, did the tasks of the house and took care of the land around the little hut, where corn and beans were planted. Gourds and chayotes grew there as well. The place where we came to live—and where I'm still living —is called Fortress Mountain, above the Mixtec section of town, very near Nindó Tocosho. My grandparents had abandoned the hut along the path to San Andrés to which, one day, Crisanto Feliciano went for his wife. Now they lived on this high place from where one could see, down there below, the little town of Huautla. There were only a few houses of thatch and shingle at that time. Trees and bushes covered everything, but the church was already built.

My grandparents told me that in their youth they had worked as servants for the priest, Catarino García. This priest lived many years in Huautla. He had children by several Indian women. At his death he asked—and it was granted—to be buried underneath the altar of the Huautla church.

Life with my grandparents was difficult. By custom we got up at dawn, when by the light of a burning *ocote* torch, Grandmother, my mother, and my aunt Juanita worked wool, silk, or cotton. The grandparents raised silkworms inside the hut; the worms took almost a year to raise. First the little butterflies laid their eggs on mats, they laid them in the month of March. At five months, the little worms came out of their little eggs and we gave them food, *mora* leaves that they ate noisily. We picked out the little worms and separated them from the bigger ones so that those didn't do them harm. The worms grew to the size of a finger. Three months after having opened their eggs, they began to drool [to leave secretions—TN], sticks were fixed up for them against the wall of the house, and on that bed of sticks they deposited the silk. It wasn't easy to raise silkworms. They required a lot of care. During the day or during the night, the silk was cleaned, the leavings of the worms were gotten rid of. They had to be fed well; if not, the worms didn't give enough or good enough silk.

Finally the silk was cleaned and gathered together. It was used to make belts that the men used as part of their clothing. From the wool and cotton, fabrics were made with which we dressed. Our life was invariable. We would wake up when the light of day was still far off. When the first rooster of the morning crowed, we were already sipping our *pinole* water sweetened with cane sugar to alleviate our hunger and cold. From time to time we drank tea made from lemon or orange leaves and only rarely coffee. My mother made the tortillas and embroidered. My grandmother and aunt worked at the primitive loom. Grandfather always hired himself out as a fieldworker, the same as an uncle of ours named Emilio Cristino.

As my sister and I grew up, our chores in the house went on growing. We took care of the chickens in the woods or gathered sticks that were used to make the fire on which the food was cooked.

I must have been eleven and my sister nine when Grandfather took us to plant corn. He made little planting stakes for us, and with those stakes we opened the hole in the ground in which we clumsily deposited the kernels of corn. The whole family went to the planting.

Sitting on the ground, María Ana and I dug with difficulty. I think the kernels fell on the surface of the ground in disorder, we were so little. In contrast, the adults sowed in a perfect line, leaving the kernels at the right depth. When the harvest drew near and the corn was tall, taller than María Ana and I, it made us laugh with joy.

If it wasn't the time of working in the fields, we were sent to take care of the chickens in the woods or two or three goats, which were finally sold. We took advantage of this time to play with our dolls that we made ourselves. One of my dolls I called Florencia José. She was a rag doll and I made her a silk *huipil.* In the house we couldn't play because my Aunt Juanita and my grandfather were too strict. They didn't like to see us playing; everything was work, work, work.

If it was a matter of planting beans, they called us. If it was a matter of planting corn, they took us there. The same at planting as at harvest.

On ordinary days, we ate beans, if there were any, or we made do with plain tortillas splashed with hot chile sauce, but on the Days of the Dead one could eat *quelite, yerba mora,* or *guasmole.*[4] On festival days, Grandfather bought beef or goat meat that Grandmother prepared in a hot stew.

The little food that Grandmother served us at dawn calmed the hunger that we had held in for a long time. I think our will to live was very great, greater than the will of many men. The will to live kept us fighting from day to day to finally get some morsel that would alleviate the hunger María Ana and I felt. Aunt Juanita hid the food, and even if my mother gave us something, hunger soon bothered us again.

---

4. [Translator's note] *Quelite* and *mora* are greens like spinach that are gathered wild. *Guasmole* is a semitropical fruit that is cooked in *tezmole.* It is abundant only in autumn.

We made efforts to hold a single mouthful in our stomachs, every evening, every morning.

Several men knew that my mother had become a widow and arrived to ask for her. They proposed to her properly: as the custom is, they arrived at dawn with *aguardiente* and chickens as a gift that they gave to my grandfather, Manuel Cosme. My mother never accepted. "My only commitment from here on will be to raise my daughters" was her reply, despite having been married only six years.

She lived with me, single, for the rest of her life.

3

Once my uncle Emilio Cristino got so sick he couldn't get up. I was a little girl of five, six, or seven. I didn't know what his sickness was. Grandmother María Estefanía, worried, went in search of a Wise Man named Juan Manuel to cure Uncle.

The Wise Man Juan Manuel, who was not a very old man, arrived at our hut after nightfall. He had a bundle wrapped up in banana leaves that he treated with exaggerated care. I went up close to see what he had in the bundle, but rapidly the Wise Man Juan Manuel took it in his hands and prevented me from getting any closer, directing an authoritarian look at me. "Nobody can look at what I have here. It isn't good: a curious look could spoil what I have here," he said. Curiosity made me stay awake. I saw how the Wise Man Juan Manuel unwrapped the banana leaves. From there he took out various big fresh mushrooms the size of a hand. I was accustomed to seeing those mushrooms in the woods where I took care of the chickens and the goats. There were many of that kind of mushroom; their brown color contrasted with the green of the pastures.

The Wise Man Juan Manuel had arrived to cure Uncle Emilio

Cristino; for the first time I witnessed a vigil with the *saint children*. I understood that later. I saw how the Wise Man Juan Manuel lit the candles and talked to the Lords of the Mountains and the Lords of the Springs. I saw how he distributed the mushrooms counting them by pairs and gave them to each of those present, including the sick person. Later, in complete darkness, he talked, talked, and talked. His language was very pretty. It pleased me. At times the Wise Man sang, sang, and sang. I didn't understand his words, but I liked them. It was a different language from what we speak in the daytime. It was a language that without my comprehending it attracted me. It was a language that spoke of stars, animals, and other things unknown to me.

A long time had gone by since it had gotten dark, and still I didn't feel sleepy. Seated very quietly on my mat, I followed the vigil attentively. One thing that I did understand, yes, was that the mushrooms had made old Juan Manuel sing. After midnight, the Wise Man lit a candle and stuck it in the ground. I saw that he danced while he said that he "saw" animals, objects, and people. No, I couldn't understand him completely. The Wise Man spoke without rest. He burned incense and rubbed "San Pedro"[5] on the forearms of the sick person.

By dawn my sick uncle, who didn't appear so sick anymore, began to sit up slowly. The Wise Man Juan Manuel animated him with his strange language. Uncle got to his feet. He hadn't done that since some days before because of his illness.

Two weeks later Uncle Emilio Cristino had recovered his health completely.

Some days after the vigil in which the Wise Man Juan Manuel cured Uncle, María Ana and I were taking care of our chickens in the

5. The name given to a ground-up tobacco (*nicotiana rustica*) mixed with lime and sometimes with garlic as well. Its use is ceremonial, and it is considered to have power against the evil influences of sorcery.

woods so that they wouldn't be the victims of hawks or foxes. We were seated under a tree when suddenly I saw near me, within reach of my hand, several mushrooms. They were the same mushrooms that the Wise Man Juan Manuel had eaten. I knew them well. My hands gently tore up one mushroom, then another. I looked at them up close. "If I eat you, you, and you, I know that you will make me sing beautifully," I said to them. I remembered that my grandparents spoke of these mushrooms with great respect. That was why I knew that they weren't bad.

Without thinking much about it, I put the mushrooms in my mouth and chewed them up. Their taste wasn't pleasant; on the contrary, they were bitter, tasting of roots, of earth. I ate them all up. My sister María Ana, watching me, did the same.

After having eaten the mushrooms, we felt dizzy, as if we were drunk, and we began to cry; but this dizziness passed and then we became very content. Later we felt good. It was like a new hope in life. That was how I felt.

In the days that followed, when we felt hungry, we ate the mushrooms. And not only did we feel our stomachs full, but content in spirit as well. The mushrooms made us ask God not to make us suffer so much. We told him that we were always hungry, that we felt cold. We didn't have anything: only hunger, only cold. I didn't know in reality whether the mushrooms were good or bad. Nor did I even know whether they were food or poison. But I felt that they spoke to me. After eating them I heard voices. Voices that came from another world. It was like the voice of a father who gives advice. Tears rolled down our cheeks, abundantly, as if we were crying for the poverty in which we lived.

Another day we ate the mushrooms and I had a vision: a well-dressed man appeared; he was as big as a tree. I heard the mysterious voice that said: "This is your father, Crisanto Feliciano...." My father. It was years since he had died, now it gave me pleasure to know him. The immense man, my father, spoke. Pointing at me he said these words: "María Sabina, kneel down. Kneel and pray...." I kneeled and prayed. I spoke to God who each time I felt to be more familiar. Closer to me. I felt as if everything that surrounded me was God. Now I felt that I spoke a lot and that my words were beautiful.

María Ana and I continued to eat the mushrooms. We ate lots, many times, I don't remember how many. Sometimes Grandfather and at other times my mother came to the woods and gathered us up from the ground where we were sprawled or kneeling. "What have you done?" they asked. They picked us up bodily and carried us home. In their arms we continued laughing, singing, or crying. They never scolded us nor hit us for eating mushrooms. Because they knew that it isn't good to scold a person who has eaten the *little things* because it could cause contrary emotions and it's possible that one might feel one was going crazy.

The next rainy season, when the mushrooms had returned, we ate them again.

Sometime later I knew that the mushrooms were like God. That they gave wisdom, that they cured illnesses, and that our people, since a long time ago, had eaten them. That they had power, that they were the blood of Christ.

Years later, when I became a widow for the second time, I gave myself up for always to wisdom, in order to cure the sicknesses of people and to be myself always close to God. One should respect the little mushrooms. At bottom I feel they are my family. As if they were my parents, my blood. In truth I was born with my destiny. To be a Wise Woman. To be a daughter of the *saint children*.

And I never went to school where I could have learned to read, to write or speak Castilian. My parents spoke only Mazatec. I never learned another language. What's more, I didn't know what school was, nor did I know it even existed; and if there had been a school I wouldn't have gone, because there wasn't time. In those days, people worked a lot.

4

By the end of our childhood, the work load had increased for María Ana and me. We had learned to make tortillas, to cook the meals, to wash, and to sweep.

One dawn, some people arrived who spoke a long time with my mother and grandparents. The people went and my mother told me that they had come to ask for me. They wanted me to unite myself in marriage with a young man. The people came once or twice, but I didn't see any marriageable young man among them; nonetheless, I met the one who was to be my husband the day he came for me. There wasn't any wedding. My mother, without consulting me, ordered me to gather my clothes together, saying that from that moment on I didn't belong to them anymore. "Now you belong to this young man who will be your husband. Go with him. Attend him well. You're a little woman ..." were her words. That is the custom.

I was fourteen. During the first days of my new life, I felt scared because I didn't know what was happening. Later I resigned myself. With the passage of time, I loved my husband very much. His name was Serapio Martínez. He was a young man of twenty. He liked to dress in clean clothes and didn't appear to be a wastrel. I found later that he was good-hearted. He didn't drink much *aguardiente,* almost none, and he didn't like to work in the fields. With pride I can say that he knew how to read and write. He dedicated himself to the commerce of the red and black thread that is used to embroider the huipils that we women wear. He also sold casseroles, plates, and cups. He traveled to Córdoba, Vera Cruz, to Tehuacán and to Puebla to buy the merchandise that he sold in Huautla or in the nearby towns. He traveled on foot at the beginning and transported the merchandise on his back. It took him eight days to go to Puebla and back. With time he succeeded in buying some pack animals on whose backs he transported what he bought there.

When I told him that I was pregnant, he took it naturally. He didn't show any feeling, neither joy nor sorrow; he barely stammered: "Then prepare yourself to be a mother." Upon returning from his travels he talked to me about the conditions of the road or spoke of the new prices of the threads or casseroles.

One time he didn't speak as usual. Upon asking him why he was silent, he answered: "I know that in Huautla they're getting people together to fight with guns. Some call themselves Carrancistas and others Zapatistas. They're going around with rifles and horses. Soon they'll come for me. They'll give me my rifle; if they see that I'm good, they'll give me a horse."

Serapio's words were fulfilled. The men of war took him away. I didn't put up any resistance.

He went when Catarino, my first child, was hardly ten days old. "Don't worry, Sabi," Serapio told me. "I'll find a way to send you some money." I watched him until I lost sight of him along the path. He went with some men who came for him. I cried a lot. But with the passing of the days, I comforted myself with the idea that he would soon return. I stayed with my mother in my little hut. My grandparents had already died; Uncle Emilio and Aunt Juanita had died as well.

The new soldiers were quartered in Huautla for several days. Afterwards they left. Serapio was named bugler at first. A year later he was a major and worked under the orders of General Adolfo Pineda,[6] who I know, Álvaro, was your grandfather. During the time that Serapio was at war, money reached me that he sent irregularly. A soldier went from house to house, leaving verbal notes, letters, and money. Serapio didn't write me because I didn't know how to read. He sent me a note only once. I looked for a person who knew how to read to tell me what was written in it. He sent to say that I shouldn't worry about him, that he was well. But on other occasions, there was neither note nor money, only the cruel news: "Serapio has died in combat." I cried. I cried on the little body of my recently born son, Catarino.

In that time the town lived in fear. We who had relatives in the war were in constant dread. A man arrived and said: "Sabi, don't afflict yourself anymore. Serapio is alive." In a little while the version changed: "Serapio is lost, nobody knows anything about him. We're confident he will appear soon." Later a hope: "Serapio has appeared." And then another disillusion: "No. He's dead." In the end I accustomed myself to this life of upsets, and there were moments when it didn't matter to me if Serapio was still alive or already dead. The rumors that arrived at my door only received a cold thank you.

But I felt my heart become big with joy when, after six months, Serapio appeared before me. At first sight I didn't recognize him. He had cartridge belts, a heavy rifle, and a military cap. He spoke very little to me about his life as a soldier, only that they had chosen him for a bugler and that when his superior died in combat, he had left the trumpet to take up the rifle of the dead soldier. What's more, they saw that he was agile. To test him they once made him run next to a horse, and they saw that he had a lot of stamina. The agile had more oppor-

6. Of Mazatec origin, Pineda was one of the leaders of the Carrancista movement in Huautla during the Mexican Revolution.

tunity to go up in rank. The agile and the valiant. Bravery came first. And Serapio was brave, his youth helped him.

Serapio went back to the war again and I didn't worry so much. He returned eight months later, not to go again. By that time my son Catarino was beginning to walk.

It's true that Serapio drank little *aguardiente* and that he worked a lot, but he liked women. He brought several loose women to my house. There were three of us under the same roof when that happened. The loose women left my house fifteen or thirty days after they arrived. I wasn't jealous because I felt myself to be Serapio's true wife. With him I had three children: Catarino, Viviana, and Apolonia. Each one of my children was born at intervals of a year and a half.

My husband's liking for women made our relations not as good as I would have liked. I loved him and it hurt me to know that he was in love with a girl in the Hot Country. He became more and more distant from me because he preferred the other.

Serapio caught the sickness of the wind [bronchial pneumonia] in the Hot Country and died after three days of agony. His pack animals and money stayed in the hands of the other woman.

Thus my marital life ended. I had a husband for six years, the same number of years that my father lived with my mother. The same as her, I became a widow at twenty.

5

I never ate the *saint children* while I lived with Serapio, since in accordance with our beliefs the woman who takes mushrooms should not have relations with men. Those who are going to stay up shouldn't have sexual relations for four days before and four days after the vigil.

Those who want to can complete five and five. I didn't take the *saint children* because I was afraid that my man wouldn't understand it. The condition should be fulfilled faithfully.

During my first years of widowhood, I felt pains from my deliveries. My waist and hips hurt me. I sent for a woman to massage me who alleviated me only a little. I also gave myself steam baths without much result. I called in a Curer and a Sucking Doctor as well but they didn't alleviate me at all. Finally I decided to take the *saint children* again. I took them alone, without recourse to any Wise One.

Those *little things* worked in my body, but I remember that the words I spoke weren't particularly good. I took them only to press my waist with my hands gently once or twice. I massaged myself in all the parts of my body where it hurt. Days went by and I got better. And I had decided to take them because I was clean. I didn't have a husband. At bottom I knew that I was a doctor woman. I knew what my destiny was. I felt it deep within me. I felt that I had a great power, a power that awakened in me in the vigils.

But in the house there was hunger. So I began to work to support my mother and my three children. Arduous constant work didn't scare me. I knew how to furrow the earth and split kindling with an axe, I knew how to plant and pick ears of corn. I worked like a strong man; sometimes I traveled to Teotitlán, where I bought pots which I resold in the market of Huautla. The raising of silkworms and the difficult work of joining wool and cotton together diminished when the merchants of Huautla began to bring cloth from the city. Since then we know muslin and colored fabrics.

In those years of my widowhood, I planted corn and beans. I also harvested coffee. On the days when I worked in the fields, I dug trenches where I deposited my little children so that they wouldn't bother me. At other times, I sold bread and candles in the ranches and the neighboring towns roundabout like San Miguel, Tenango, or Río Santiago.

6

Some years, I don't know how many, after I became a widow for the first time, my sister María Ana got sick. She felt pains in her stomach; they were sharp stabs that made her double up and groan from pain. Each time I saw her she was worse. If she felt more or less well, she began her housework; but, without her being able to control herself, there came a moment when she fainted in the path.

Her fainting spells occurred more frequently later.

With great fear for her health, I contracted Curers to heal her, but I could see with anxiety that her illness got worse. One morning she didn't get up from her bed; she trembled and groaned. I felt preoccupied as never before. I called various Curers but it was useless; they couldn't cure my sister.

That afternoon, seeing my sister stretched out, I imagined her dead. My only sister. No, that couldn't be. She couldn't die. I knew that the *saint children* had the power. I had eaten them as a little girl and remembered that they didn't do harm. I knew that our people ate them to heal their sicknesses. So I made a decision; that same night I would take the holy mushrooms. I did it. To her I gave three pairs. I ate many in order for them to give me immense power. I can't lie: I must have eaten thirty pairs of the "landslide" variety.

When the *children* were working inside my body, I prayed and asked God to help me cure María Ana. Little by little I felt that I could speak with more and more facility. I went close to the sick woman. The *saint children* guided my hands to press her hips. Softly I massaged her where she said it hurt. I spoke and sang. I felt that I sang beautifully. I said what those *children* obliged me to say.

I went on pressing my sister, her stomach and her hips. Finally a lot of blood came out. Water and blood as if she were giving birth. I didn't get frightened because I knew that the *Little-One-Who-Springs-Forth* was curing her through me. Those *saint children* gave me advice and I carried it out. I attended my sister until the bleeding stopped. Afterward she left off groaning and slept. My mother sat down next to her to attend to her.

I couldn't sleep. The little *saints* continued working in my body. I remember that I had a vision: some people appeared who inspired me with respect. I knew they were the Principal Ones of whom my ancestors spoke. They were seated behind a table on which there were many written papers. I knew that they were important papers. There were a number of Principal Ones, six or eight of them. Some looked at me, others read the papers on the table, others appeared to be searching for something among the same papers. I knew that they weren't of flesh and bone. I knew that they weren't beings of water or tortilla. I knew that it was a revelation that the *saint children* were giving me. Right away I heard a voice. A voice that was sweet but authoritarian at the same time. Like the voice of a father who loves his children but raises them strictly. A wise voice that said: "These are the Principal Ones." I understood that the mushrooms were speaking to me. I felt an infinite happiness. On the Principal Ones' table a book appeared, an open book that went on growing until it was the size of a person. In its pages there were letters. It was a white book, so white it was resplendent.

One of the Principal Ones spoke to me and said: "María Sabina, this is the Book of Wisdom. It is the Book of Language. Everything that is written in it is for you. The Book is yours, take it so that you can work." I exclaimed with emotion: "That is for me. I receive it."

The Principal Ones disappeared and left me alone in front of the immense Book. I knew that it was the Book of Wisdom.

The Book was before me, I could see it but not touch it. I tried to caress it but my hands didn't touch anything. I limited myself to contemplating it and, at that moment, I began to speak. Then I realized that I was reading the Sacred Book of Language. My Book. The Book of the Principal Ones.

I had attained perfection. I was no longer a simple apprentice. For that, as a prize, as a nomination, the Book had been granted me. When one takes the *saint children,* one can see the Principal Ones.[7] Otherwise not. And it's because the mushrooms are saints; they give wisdom. Wisdom is Language. Language is in the Book. The Book is granted by the Principal Ones. The Principal Ones appear through the great power of the *children.*

I learned the wisdom of the Book. Afterward, in my later visions, the Book no longer appeared because I already had its contents in my memory.

The vigil in which I cured my sister María Ana I conducted as the ancient Mazatecs did. I used candles of pure wax; flowers, white lilies and gladiolas (all kinds of flowers can be used as long as they have scent and color); copal and San Pedro as well.

In a brazier I burned the copal and with the smoke incensed the *saint children* that I held in my hands. Before eating them, I spoke to

7. According to the explanations that old people in Huautla have given me, the Principal Ones are persons who head a municipal office or else it is the title that is given to persons who have important posts. With respect to the visions of María Sabina, the Principal Ones are the personification of the mushrooms she has eaten. The mushrooms turn into people who handle important papers.

them. I asked them for favor. That they bless us, that they teach us the way, the truth, the cure. That they give us the power to follow the tracks of evil in order to be done with it. I said to the mushrooms: "I will take your blood. I will take your heart. Because my conscience is pure, it is clean like yours. Give me truth. May Saint Peter and Saint Paul be with me." When I felt dizzy, I blew out the candles. The darkness serves as a background for what is seen.

In that same vigil, after the Book disappeared, I had another vision: I saw the Supreme Lord of the Mountains, Chicon Nindó. I saw a man on horseback come toward my hut. I knew—the voice told me—that that being was an important person. His mount was beautiful: a white horse, white as foam. A beautiful horse.

The personage reined up his mount at the door of my hut. I could see him through the walls. I was inside the house but my eyes had the power to see through any obstacle. The personage waited for me to go out.

With decision I went out to meet him. I stood next to him.

Yes, it was Chicon Nindó, he who lives on Nindó Tocosho, he who is the Lord of the Mountains. He who has the power to enchant spirits. He who himself cures the sick. To whom turkeys are sacrificed, to whom the Curers give cacao in order for him to cure.

I stood next to him and went closer. I saw that he didn't have a face though he wore a white sombrero. His face, yes, his face was like a shadow.

The night was black; the clouds covered the sky but Chicon Nindó was like a being covered by a halo. I became mute.

Chicon Nindó didn't say a word. All of a sudden he set his mount into motion to continue on his way. He disappeared along the path, in the direction of his dwelling place: the enormous Mountain of the Adoration, Nindó Tocosho. He lives there, while I live on Fortress

Mountain, the closest one to Nindó Tocosho. That makes us neighbors. Chicon Nindó had come because in my wise Language I had called him.

I entered the house and had another vision: I saw that something fell from the sky with a great roar, like a lightning bolt. It was a luminous object that blinded. I saw that it fell through a hole in one of the walls. The fallen object turned into a kind of vegetal being, covered by a halo like Chicon Nindó's. It was like a bush with flowers of many colors; in its head it had a great radiance. Its body was covered with leaves and stalks. There it stood, in the center of the hut. I looked straight at it. Its arms and legs were like branches and it was soaked with freshness and behind it appeared a red background. The vegetal being lost itself in this red background until it disappeared completely. When the vision vanished, I was sweating, sweating. My sweat wasn't warm but cool. I realized that I was crying and that my tears were crystals that tinkled when they fell on the ground. I went on crying but I whistled and clapped, sounded and danced. I danced because I knew that I was the great Clown woman and the Lord clown woman. At dawn I slept placidly. I slept, but it wasn't a deep sleep; rather I felt that I was rocking in a reverie . . . as if my body were swaying in a gigantic hammock, suspended from the sky, which swung between the mountains.

I woke up when the world was already in sunlight. It was morning, I touched my body and the ground to make sure that I had returned to the world of humans. I was no longer near the Principal Ones. Seeing what surrounded me, I looked for my sister María Ana. She was asleep. I didn't want to wake her. I also saw that a part of the walls of the hut had fallen down, that another was about to fall. Now I believe that while the *saint children* worked in my body, I myself knocked over the wall with the weight of my body. I suppose that when I danced I hit against the wall and toppled it over. In the following days the people who passed asked what had happened to the house. I limited myself to telling them that the rains and winds of the last few days had weakened the mud-wattled walls and finally overthrown them.

And María Ana got better. She was healed once and for all. To this day she lives in good health with her husband and her children near Santa Cruz de Juárez.

From that cure on I had faith in the *saint children*. People realized how difficult it was to cure my sister. Many people learned of it and in a few days they came in search of me. They brought their sick. They came from places far away. I cured them with the Language of the *children*. The people came from Tenango, Río Santiago, or San Juan Coatzospan. The sick arrived looking pale, but the mushrooms told me what the remedy was. They advised me what to do to cure them. People have continued to seek me. And since I received the Book I have become one of the Principal Ones. If they appear, I sit down with them and we drink beer or *aguardiente*. I have been among them since the time when, gathered together behind a table with important papers, they gave me wisdom, the perfect word: the Language of God.

Language makes the dying return to life. The sick recover their health when they hear the words taught by the *saint children*. There is no mortal who can teach this Language.

After I had cured my sister María Ana, I understood that I had found my path. The people knew it and came to me to cure their sick. In search of a cure came those who had been enchanted by elves, those who had lost their spirit from fright in the woods, at the river, or along the path. For some there was no remedy and they died. I cure with Language, the Language of the *saint children*. When they advise me to sacrifice chickens, they are placed on the parts where it hurts. The rest is Language. But my path to wisdom was soon to be cut off.

7

Twelve years after I became a widow, a man named Marcial Carrera began to woo me. Really, I didn't have any need for a man because I knew how to support myself. I knew how to work; my family, at least, didn't suffer as much as I had. There was hunger, yes, but it wasn't as burning as what María Ana and I had experienced. My work helped each one have something to eat and something to wear.

Marcial Carrera insisted. In accordance with the custom, he brought his parents to speak with my mother. My mother persuaded me to accept that man. She said that a man in the house would help to make my work less heavy. The days passed and I thought about it because my suitor didn't appear to be a worker. What's more, he had the reputation of being irresponsible and a drunk.

But in the end I gave in. I stated my conditions: if Marcial wanted a woman, he would have to come to live in my house because I wasn't going to move my mother, my children, my mat, my pots, my hoes, and my machetes to his. It seemed to me that my house was better than poor Marcial's.

Marcial accepted my conditions and he came to live in my house. With time, I found that Marcial drank a lot of *aguardiente*. He was a Curer. He used turkey eggs and macaw feathers to do sorcery.

He hit me frequently and made me cry. He didn't like to work in the fields and didn't even know how to use a hoe with dexterity.

As I saw that Marcial earned little money, that it wasn't enough to cover the small expenses of the house, I was forced to return to work. I went back to retailing bread and candles.

In the thirteen years that I lived with Marcial I had six children. They died, all of them; only my daughter Aurora survived. My children died from sickness or were murdered. While I lived with Mar-

cial I never took the *saint children*. I feared that he wouldn't under-
stand me and would spoil my Wise Woman's bodily cleanliness.

Marcial, the same as my first husband, Serapio, liked other women.
The sons of a lady with whom he had relations beat him up and
wounded him with a machete. Bleeding, he died sprawled in the path.

8

The fact of having become a widow for the second time made it eas-
ier, in a way, for me to decide to give myself up to my destiny. The
destiny that had been fixed for me from before I was born: to be a
Wise Woman. My destiny was to cure. To cure with the Language of
the *saint children*. I determined to do this even though I had to go on
working hard to support my family—now not as much, though, be-
cause my son Catarino was already beginning to work. He dealt in
thread that he resold in the Hot Country, following in the footsteps of
his deceased father.

I'm not sure, but I believe I was then more than forty years old. I
didn't feel in a condition to travel to sell bread and candles in the
ranches. During the time that I lived with my husband Marcial,
I saved up enough to build a house seven arm-lengths long, with
wooden walls and a thatched roof of sugarcane leaves. The house was
alongside the path to San Miguel. In it I set up a store in which I sold
aguardiente and cigarettes. Afterward I sold meals there to travelers.

In the days after my second widowhood, I wanted to practice cur-
ing as Marcial had done. I felt that I should cure and that I should cure
with the *saint children,* but something made me hold back. As if it was
fear to give oneself up to what has been given one, to what has been
destined.

I tried being a Curer, yes, but it didn't satisfy me.

My feelings were that I was doing what I shouldn't do. I thought that the clean woman, the woman of Christ, the Morning Star woman, shouldn't practice being a Curer. I was destined to something superior. In curing I buried eggs as an offering to the Lords of the Mountains. I buried them at the corners of the house or inside, but I saw that worms came out where I buried them, and that caused me disgust and horror. I thought that this was not my destined path. I remembered my ancestors. My great-grandfather Juan Feliciano, my grandfather Pedro Feliciano, my great-aunt María Ana Jesús, and my great-uncle Antonio Justo had all been Wise Ones of great prestige.

9

For me sorcery and curing are inferior tasks. The Sorcerers and Curers have their Language as well, but it is different from mine. They ask favors from Chicon Nindó. I ask them from God the Christ, from Saint Peter, from Magdalene and Guadalupe.

It's that in me there is no sorcery, there is no anger, there are no lies. Because I don't have garbage, I don't have dust. The sickness comes out if the sick vomit. They vomit the sickness. They vomit because the mushrooms want them to. If the sick don't vomit, I vomit. I vomit for them and in that way the malady is expelled. The mushrooms have power because they are the flesh of God. And those that believe are healed. Those that do not believe are not healed.

The people who realized that I cured María Ana brought their sick children. One, two, ten, many. I have cured many children. Sometimes I give the children a little bit of *Little-One-Who-Springs-Forth*. I vomit for the children if they don't. Before beginning the vigil I ask the name of the sick person. In that way I search for the sickness and in that way I cure. If the sick person doesn't tell me the cause of his or her malady I divine it. When the sick person sweats, that reveals that he or she is going to be healed. Sweat gets rid of the fever that comes from the sickness. My words oblige the evil to leave.

For a strong toothache seven or eight pairs are eaten, that is enough. The children are taken at night; the vigil is celebrated in front of images of the saints of the Church. The *saint children* cure the sores, the wounds of the spirit. The spirit is what gets sick. The Curers don't know that the visions the children show reveal the origin of the malady. The Curers don't know how to use them. The Sorcerers don't either. The Sorcerers are afraid of Wise Ones like me because they know that I can discover if they have caused an enchantment, if they have surreptitiously robbed the spirit of a child, of a man, or of a woman. The mushrooms give me the power of universal contemplation. I can see from the origin. I can arrive where the world is born.

The sick person gets well and the relatives come to visit me afterward to tell me that there has been an alleviation. They thank me with *aguardiente,* cigarettes, or some coins. I am not a Curer because I do not use eggs to cure. I don't ask for powers from the Lords of the Mountains. I am not a Curer because I do not give potions of strange herbs to drink. I cure with Language. Nothing else. I am not a Sorceress because I don't do evil. I am a Wise Woman. Nothing else.

Men come as well to ask me to help their women give birth. I am a midwife, but that is not my work. I am the one who speaks with God and with Benito Juárez. I am wise even from within the womb of my mother. I am the woman of the winds, of the water, of the paths, because I am known in heaven, because I am a doctor woman.

I take *Little-One-Who-Springs-Forth* and I see God. I see him sprout from the earth. He grows and grows, big as a tree, as a mountain. His face is placid, beautiful, serene as in the temples. At other times, God is not like a man: he is the Book. A Book that is born from the earth, a sacred Book whose birth makes the world shake. It is the Book of God that speaks to me in order for me to speak. It counsels me, it teaches me, it tells me what I have to say to men, to the sick, to life. The Book appears and I learn new words.

I am the daughter of God and elected to be wise. On the altar that I have in my house is the image of Our Lady of Guadalupe. I have her in a niche. And I also have Saint Mark, Saint Martin Horseman, and Saint Magdalene. They help me to cure and to speak. In the vigils I clap and whistle; at that time I am transformed into God.

10

One day a couple came to my house. I was inside near the hearth, heating my tortillas. A dog barked and I went out to see what it was. I invited the visitors to come in. I interrupted my meal and attended to them.

"We're family of old Francisco García," said the man.

"The Francisco who lives in Backbone-of-a-Dog?" I asked. "What brings you here?"

"Yes. There is something, that's why we've come to see you," said the woman. "Probably you know that my father Francisco is sick."

"What caused his illness?"

"We don't know," the man went on. "We can only say that he left for his field one morning, but he soon returned before it was completely daylight. His right shinbone was hurt. He said that he was hoeing when he felt a terrible pain in the shinbone that made him fall and lose consciousness. When he came to, he returned painfully to his house. He supposes that he hit himself with the hoe. To heal him we've contracted the young doctor who has just arrived in Huautla from the city. He is a Wise-One-In-Medicine who cures bloody wounds. He's been treating old Francisco for days, but Francisco doesn't appear to be getting better. We've decided that you, yes, would know how to heal him; you would contribute a lot together with the medicine from the young doctor. The *little things* will give strength to old Francisco and he will get well quickly....You are a woman who knows, María Sabina."

"When do you want to do the vigil?" I asked.

"As soon as possible," the man ended by saying.

The couple went. I said that that same night I would go to old Francisco García.

At nightfall I arrived at their hut. They treated me with great respect. They took me to the bed of old Francisco who lay on a mat and groaned from pain. The old man saw me and made an effort to smile. He had circles under his eyes. I examined the supposed wound in the shinbone. It looked more like a bruise without serious complications.

I began the ceremony in front of the images of the saints that the family had. I gave old Francisco six pairs of mushrooms. I took thirteen pairs. Other people who were present also took their pairs. I let myself be carried away. I didn't offer any resistance and I fell into a deep, interminable well. I felt a kind of vertigo. Gradually the discomfort disappeared. I had a vision: I saw a tiger about to attack one of several cattle in a corral. It was night. The animal, crouched, chest to the ground, prepared to spring and pounce on its prey, when the strong blow of a stone in its right leg stopped it. The stone had been thrown by a man in a nearby tree. The tiger fled without having accomplished its purpose, wounded and frightened.

Next a woman appeared who covered her face with her forearm so that it wouldn't be seen that she was smiling. It was a smile of satisfaction. I recognized the woman. She was the wife of Faustino Méndez, a sorceress. The voice of the mushrooms said: "She bewitched old Francisco: she turned his spirit into a tiger. It is her."

Past midnight old Francisco started to sit up little by little. By himself, without help. Finally he got completely to his feet. Erect, he stood next to the altar where the images of the saints were. He made movements as if to relax. I asked, then, that they bring him clean clothes. What he had on was contaminated. He should change because the cure was approaching, and everything dirty should be shed.

I ordered old Francisco to sit down on the chair and I asked him: "The day that you hurt yourself, where was it? What happened? Didn't you feel that your body didn't have a spirit? That your body was empty? What places do you go to in your dreams?"

"Yes, Señora," he answered, looking at the ground as if he felt ashamed. "For some time now, my dreams are regularly the same. No sooner do I go to sleep than I dream that I'm coming to a corral where I see bulls. I want to attack the animals to eat them."

"What places have you arrived at?"

"I dream that I'm in Ojitlán. It's there I want to attack the cattle."

"Don't be ashamed," I told him. "There's definitely nothing wrong with that. It's not a lie. When we sleep the spirit leaves the body and wanders. It goes where it wants to go. The spirit returns if we wake up. But some people are born with their 'fate.' Their spirit turns into an opossum, a tiger, or a buzzard. Transformed into animals they travel to distant places. If you have a 'fate' don't worry. It is not a sin nor anything to be ashamed of. There are people who are born like that; others can get to have a 'fate' by the artifices of sorcery."[8]

---

8. Here María Sabina uses her own word *soerte* (a deformation of the Spanish word *suerte,* "luck") for what students of pre-Hispanic and colonial Mexico call *nagual* (or a phenomenon related to *nagualism:* the *tona*). For María Sabina the *soerte,* translated here as "fate," is the spirit of a person, capable of leaving the human body to turn itself into an animal, usually a tiger.

"Yes," he continued, "I dream that I prowl around the cattle. I hear their bellows. It happens to me every night."

The *little things* ordered me to light a candle. I took a little San Pedro with my fingers and ordered old Francisco to chew it. He did. He swallowed the San Pedro. I asked the people around me to bring a basin. They brought it. Then I asked them to press old Francisco's stomach so that he would vomit. He vomited. San Pedro made him do it. The tobacco is called San Pedro because that saint created it.

I ordered old Francisco to change his clothes when he finished vomiting.

At dawn the sick man spoke: "I thank you for your cure, María Sabina. I feel better. I'm hungry. Very ..." They served him coffee, a little bit of roasted meat, beans, and chile sauce. He ate well and abundantly.

I spoke to him once more:

"The *saint children* have revealed that a sorceress has turned your spirit into a tiger. At night, while you sleep, your 'fate' goes to attack the bulls of Ojitlán. Don't be worried anymore. The mushrooms have already cured you. You've vomited."

Although I knew that the young Wise-One-In-Medicine continued to see the patient, I was sure that the mushrooms would remedy his malady. Within a month they let me know that old Francisco was completely recovered.

The wife of Faustino Méndez, the sorceress, began to go crazy the moment Francisco vomited. That way the "fate" came out and Francisco recaptured his spirit. The sorceress, crazed, would take off all her clothes and go out into the street naked. Her husband and her children left her from shame and fear. The family fell into misfortune. Finally the lady died of insanity. Her evil turned against her.

The following year a daughter of old Francisco came to see me. Once inside my house she said: "All my family send you greetings. The people who visit my father ask who cured him. He tells them he has a doctor, insignificant in appearance, named María Sabina."

"Is something the matter now?" I asked.

"Señora, you know how life is. Sicknesses come and go. A child gets sick just as well as an adult. It's always happening. I've come because my nephew, Rodrigo, is sick. The young Wise-One-In-Medicine from the city has been giving him medicine, but he isn't getting any better. We're agreed that you, Señora, should cure him once and for all."

"What's the matter with him?" I asked.

"The priest Alfonso asked for him to be an apostle last Holy Week. Ezequiel, his father, accepted, because it pleased him that his son Rodrigo should be an apostle. In Holy Week the people and the apostles went in procession, but Rodrigo tripped at the door of the church and fell. It's been two months already that the child can't get up. The Sorcerers have gone with cacao and eggs to pay the places where the child was accustomed to play. We believe that he was enchanted by the master of some sacred place and that now there's no cure."

"Don't worry, woman," I told her. "I'll go tomorrow."

The following night I presented myself at the house of Ezequiel, taking enough *saint children* for six people.

I probed the body of the child with my fingers in the light of a candle. He didn't have any wound, but in a little while I'd know the true sickness.

The people of the house accompanied me in taking *Little-One-Who-Springs-Forth* ... and when it was working, I had a vision: I saw

Rodrigo walking in the midst of a crowd. He had a robe on. A purple robe like the one the apostles wear. The child walked solemnly. But his spirit wasn't with him, it was somewhere else; that's what the voice told me, and in that way I learned that a spirit who carried a rifle fired a shot and accidentally hit the spirit of Rodrigo. At that instant the child fell at the door of the church. His spirit was wounded, but his body wasn't.

When the vision had passed I lit a taper, lifted up the little shirt of the boy and saw in his chest, around the region of the heart, a hole the size of a fist. It was a wound without blood even though it was deep. When I looked at Rodrigo's face, he looked dead. So I asked for thirteen cacao beans, ground up and mixed with water.

I asked for thirteen cacao beans because my thought ordered me to. I asked as well for a recently born chick and a cloth to use as a bandage. I sacrificed the chick and bathed its still warm body in chocolate water and put it on Rodrigo's chest. On top of it I put the bandage, wrapping it around Rodrigo's body. The child didn't take *Little-One-Who-Springs-Forth.* By dawn the effect had worn off, and I took off the bandage together with the chick in the light of day. I didn't see the wound that I had seen in the sick one's chest while the *saint children* worked inside me.

The chick was buried near the house so that it wouldn't be eaten by birds of prey or by dogs. What is used in a vigil is sacred and shouldn't be spoiled by being eaten by an animal.

I slept in the house. When I awoke, they gave me food and I started to talk with the mother of the sick child. Someone came in and announced that the young Wise-One-In-Medicine, the same one who had tried to cure old Francisco, the grandfather of Rodrigo, was waiting outside to be received and to see his patient.

I saw the Wise-One-In-Medicine enter. I was seated on the ground with my legs drawn up underneath me, leaning against the wall. He was dressed in white, clean clothes. He said the Mazatec greeting to everyone: *Nina'ti'?ntali* ("In the name of God good day"). We responded in the same way.

We all kept silent while he went over the sick child with his metals. Nobody told him that that same night there had been a vigil in order for me to cure the child. He spoke in Castilian with Ezequiel, the father of Rodrigo. I didn't understand anything. He gave him some little boxes and a paper.

The young Wise Man had a white face and blue eyes. He took leave of everyone: "*Xt?alanca',*" he said to each one. He had learned to shake hands like the Mazatecs: he just grazed his fingers against the other person's palm like we do.

At bottom I didn't know what to think about the efficacy of his medicines. What I was sure of, though, was that he, with all his wisdom, ignored the true cause of the child Rodrigo's sickness.

I took leave of the sick one's parents. I told them that their child was cured ... that by the end of several days the child would be completely healthy. As payment they gave me a pack of cigarettes, a little *aguardiente,* and five pesos.

A Wise One like me should not charge for her services. She should not profit from her wisdom. The one who charges is a liar. The Wise One is born to cure, not to do business with her knowledge.... One receives with humility the two or three pesos that are put in one's hand. Yes ... one should not make money from the *little things*.

Time went by. One day I went down to the market in Huautla. I went by to say hello to Rodrigo's father. He greeted me, smiling. Very contented.

"How is the child?" I asked Ezequiel.

"He's all better. He's already playing with his little friends again.

Thank you for curing him. Because you know, you can. Thank you. Take two pesos to buy bread."

"Don't say that, Ezequiel," I answered, "because the one who has healed your son is God who is raising all of us."

From then on, old Francisco and Ezequiel, his son, had a lot of faith in me, and whenever there was someone sick in their house they called me to cure them.

1 2

During my vigils I speak to the saints: to Lord Santiago, to Saint Joseph, and to Mary. I say the name of each one as they appear.

I know that God is formed by all the saints. Just as we, together, form humanity, God is formed by all the saints. That is why I don't have a preference for any one saint. All the saints are equal, one has the same force as the other, none has more power than another.

I know of other Wise Ones who use the *saint children* as I do. I remember Toribio García, a man of this same section, who lived along the path down below. He searched for light in the *children,* but he also sought the answer in thirteen kernels of corn that he threw on the ground. The final position of each kernel has a meaning. Like that he divined what he desired. I don't practice that type of thing: I only trust in what the *children* tell me. For me that is sufficient; my only force is my Language. Toribio was another type of Wise One. He cast kernels of corn during the vigil. At dawn he repeated the throw of chance.

During the time that I was married I didn't utilize the services of Toribio. The children of my first marriage grew up healthy.

And if I get sick now, I cure myself. The *children* cure me. I've been able to live many years ... many ... I don't know how many.

In my vigils I can see how our little Christ is. I contemplate him. I can have him very close to me, but I can't touch him. There are times when I want to catch what I see with my hands, but there is nothing there and on occasions that makes me laugh. I enter another world different from the one we know in the daylight. It is a beautiful world but an unattainable one. It is like watching the movies. I know the movies because one day a man came and took me to the center of Huautla to see a film in which I appear. In the movies one can see from a distance, but if one tries one can't touch anything that one is seeing. As in the movies, after one image comes another. Then something else comes out and afterward still something else. That is how I feel the effect of the *little things*.

In that way I see the saints. One appears and I pronounce his name; if another appears, I pronounce his name. If Benito Juárez appears, I pronounce his name. Sometimes the Principal Ones appear, then I see myself drinking beer with them; at other times we drink *aguardiente*. I see animals such as gigantic serpents, but I don't fear them. I don't fear them because they are also creatures of God. Strange animals appear such as have never been seen in this world. Nothing that the mushrooms show should be feared.

And all my Language is in the Book[9] that was given to me. I am she who reads, the interpreter. That is my privilege. Although the Language is not the same for different cases. If I'm curing a sick person, I use one type of Language. If the only aim in taking the *little things* is to encounter God, then I use another Language. Now, sober, I can remember something of my Language:

I am a woman who was born alone, says
I am a woman who fell out by herself, says

9. In speaking of the Book she uses the Spanish word *Libro*.

Because your Book exists, says
Your Book of Wisdom, says
Your sacred Language, says
Your communion wafer that is given me, says
Your communion wafer that I share, says

In what number do you rest, beloved Father?
Father full of life
Father full of freshness

I am a woman of battles
Because I am a woman general, says
Because I am a woman corporal, says
I am a sergeant woman, says
I am a commander woman, says

You Jesus Christ
You Mary
You Holy Father
Woman saint
Woman saintess
Spirit woman
I am a woman who waits, says
I am a daylight woman
I am a Moon woman, says
I am a Morning Star woman
I am a God Star woman

I am the Constellation of the Sandal woman, says
I am the Staff Constellation woman, says
Here I bring my dew
My freshness
Here I bring my dew
My transparent dew, says

Because I am a fresh dew woman, says
I am a moist dew woman, says
I am the woman of the dawn, says
I am the woman of the day, says
I am the saint woman, says
I am the spirit woman, says
I am the woman who works, says
I am the woman beneath the dripping tree, says
I am the woman of the twilight, says
I am the woman of the pristine huipil, says
I am the whirlpool woman, says
I am the woman who looks into the insides of things, says
Because I can speak with Benito Juárez
Because our beautiful Virgin accompanies me
Because we can go up to heaven
I am the woman who sees Benito Juárez
Because I am the lawyer woman
Because I am the pure woman
I am the woman of goodness
Because I can go in and out of the realm of death
Because I come searching beneath the water from the opposite shore
Because I am the woman who springs forth
I am the woman who can be torn up, says
I am the doctor woman, says
I am the herb woman, says
And our beautiful Virgin Guadalupe
And our Mother Magdalene
Because I am the daughter of God
I am the daughter of Christ
I am the daughter of Mary
I am the daughter of Saint Joseph and of the Candelaria

That is part of my Language. The ignorant could never sing like
the wise. The *saint children* dictate to me, I am the interpreter. The

Book appears and there I begin to read. I read without stammering. The Book doesn't always appear because I keep in memory what is written in it.

For the sick there is one type of Language, for those who search for God there is another. For the sick, the Language appears when I am near them. I am always next to the sick one, attentive to whether the person vomits or to whatever happens. The sick get well quickly if they chew San Pedro. If the sick chew San Pedro, I say:

I am a Saint Peter woman, says
I am a Saint Paul woman, says
I am a woman who searches beneath the water, says
I am a woman who cleans with herbs, says
I am the woman who cleans, says
I am the woman who fixes things, says
I am the woman who swims, says
I am the sacred swimmer, says
I am the Lord swimmer, says
I am the greatest swimmer, says
I am the launch woman, says
I am the Morning Star woman, says

The *little things* are the ones who speak. If I say: "I am a woman who fell out by herself, I am a woman who was born alone," the *saint children* are the ones who speak. And they say that because they spring up by themselves. Nobody plants them. They spring up because God wants them to. For that reason I say: "I am the woman who can be torn up," because the *children* can be torn up and taken. They should be taken just as they are picked. They shouldn't be boiled or anything. It's not necessary to do anything more to them. As they are pulled up from the ground they should be eaten, dirt and all. They should be eaten completely, because if a piece is thrown away from carelessness, the *children* ask when they are working: "Where are my feet? Why didn't you eat me all up?" And they order: "Look for the rest of my body and take me." The words of the *children* should be obeyed. One has to look for the bits that weren't eaten before beginning the vigil and take them.

1 3

Marcial, my second husband, died, and I dedicated myself to work. I sold food in my house of seven arm-lengths situated at the side of the path. I went to San Miguel or to Tenango to sell candles and bread on market days and festival days. I lived tranquilly with my children. Although already married, my daughters Viviana and Apolonia visited me frequently.

One month after Marcial died, I began to take the *little things*. As I've already said, it isn't good to use the *children* when one has a husband. When one goes to bed with a man their cleanliness is spoiled. If a man takes them and two or three days afterwards he uses a woman, his testicles rot. If a woman does the same, she goes crazy.

Problems have not been lacking. One day a drunk entered my little store. He came on horseback. He entered with his horse. Inside he dismounted and asked for a beer. I served him the beer. My son Catarino, already a man, was inside the house. The drunk saw him.

"Ah, are you here, Catarino?" he asked.

"Yes, Crescencio," said my son. "I brought some merchandise for my mother to sell in her little store. I've just come from the Hot Country, from the town of Río Sapo. I brought two ninety-two-pound sacks of dried fish and some beans."

"Would you like to have a drink?" asked the drunk.

"I accept," answered Catarino. "We know how to drink."

"Serve us, Señora," the drunk ordered me. "Serve Catarino a glass of *aguardiente*."

Before I could serve, Catarino spoke:

"No, Crescencio, I won't drink *aguardiente*. If there weren't any beers, I'd drink *aguardiente*, but there are beers. I won't drink the *aguardiente* you're inviting me to. Open two beers, Mamá," ordered my son.

At that moment the drunk pulled a pistol out of his belt. I was afraid for my son. The drunk spoke:

"Is it true what you're saying, Catarino?" he asked, pistol in hand.

With apparent rage, he went up to my son.

"God knows whether you're a bandit or not," he added.

"Don't blaspheme, Crescencio," said my son, keeping calm. "I'm a working man. I earn my living bringing merchandise from Puebla and Mexico. It seems to me you're the bandit."

They went on talking, challenging each other.

The drunk staggered, pistol in hand. Behind him I glimpsed a crucifix; at that I got brave and interposed myself between the drunk and my son who was on my left. I went up cautiously; the drunk continued cursing. In a careless moment on the man's part, I wrested the pistol from him.

"Why have you come to fight here?" I asked. "You shouldn't do it here, because God is present here in my house."

The drunk didn't say anything more. I put the pistol in a drawer underneath the table on which I put the beers. Angry, I went up to the drunk and shoved him out. But with a push he threw me to the ground and took the opportunity to run to the drawer and grab hold of the pistol. I ran and got between them to protect my son. Determined, the drunk came up to me.

"Stop, the Sacred Heart is in my hands," I shouted at him. In a moment I felt myself sprawled on the ground bleeding at the waist: two shots had hit me in the right buttock and another in the hip on the same side.

They took me on a stretcher to the center of Huautla. They took me to the young Wise-One-In-Medicine. I learned that his name was Salvador Guerra. He took out the bullets. On that occasion the doctor met me. For the first time in my life I was cured by a Wise-One-In-Medicine. I was amazed. Before operating he injected a substance in the region where I was wounded and my pains disappeared. While he cured me I didn't feel any pain; after he finished he showed me the bullets. Thankful and amazed, I told him: "Doctor, you are great like I am. You make pain disappear. You took the bullets out of me and I didn't feel anything."

Three days later I returned to my house. I wanted to drink coffee, to eat tortillas and chile sauce. I wanted to savor my own cooking. The food that the Wise-Man-In-Medicine's helpers gave me, it was hard for me to get down.

One afternoon, while I was in my house, a man arrived to tell me that that same night Salvador Guerra himself would arrive with a foreign lady who wanted to meet me. I prepared myself for a vigil.

At night, the young Wise Man arrived in his metal [jeep] with a blonde lady. A translator told me that only the lady would take the *little saints*. I didn't pay any attention, I prepared several pairs of *little birds* for the Wise-Man-In-Medicine. When the time came, I spoke to him in Mazatec telling him to eat the *children* with me. I stretched out my hand to give them to him. With brusque gestures he refused to take them. So I said to him: "You gave me the medicine with which you cure the wounded. You healed me. You took out my bullets. Now

I offer you my medicine. Take these pairs as payment for your services." The blonde woman backed up my words. Finally the young Wise Man took his pairs of the "landslide" variety.

From then on, Salvador Guerra and I were good friends. Later our friendship became firmer and the day he left Huautla [in 1960] the priest, Alfonso Aragón, gave a mass to ask for a long life for all of us. Salvador Guerra and I kneeled in front of the altar.

When the mass was over, I offered him my hand and said to him, "Doctor!" He reciprocated by giving me his hand, saying: "Doctor!"

And now, when I see that drunk who wounded me cross my path, I greet him. Poor fellow, he's fallen apart ... he's a useless man. His drunkenness has finished him off.

1 4

A few years before the first foreigners I met arrived in Huautla, a neighbor, Guadalupe, the wife of [the *síndico*][10] Cayetano García, came to my house.

"I've had an ugly dream," she said. "I want you to come to the house to see about us. I don't feel well. I'm asking you as a favor. It's possible that problems are approaching for my husband because his office as *síndico* is difficult. You know, Señora, that there is violence in the town. There are envies. For nothing at all people hurt and kill each other. There are discords."

"I'll go with you right now," I told her.

Upon arriving at their house, Cayetano invited me to sit down. He

10. In Mexican town government, the *síndico* is the representative of the district attorney (Ministerio Público) wherever, as in Huautla, there is no district attorney's office. Cayetano García was *síndico* from 1953 to 1955.

took another chair. His wife did the same. In a discreet voice, the *síndico* spoke:

"I know who you are, María Sabina. That's why I've sent for you. We have faith in you. You've cured those who have been ill here in the house, but now I'm going to ask you something special. I want you to be my adviser. The town has elected me to municipal office. You know that to be one of the authorities is a big responsibility. You have to make decisions and you can make mistakes. So I ask you to advise me and guide me, because you have power; you know, you can know the truth no matter how hidden it is because the *little things* teach you. If there are any problems of litigation in the municipality, you will tell me where the guilt lies and I, as *síndico,* will say what should be done."

"Don't worry," I answered him. "We'll do what you ask. I can't say no because we're old friends and because I obey the authorities. What's more I know that you're a good man. I don't doubt it. I will be your adviser. We'll consult the *saint children* as many times as it's necessary."

Cayetano García was *síndico* for three years; in that time there were no serious problems or situations that the town government could lament.

But I should tell the incident that preceded the arrival of the first foreigners who came to me. More or less fifteen days after the drunk wounded me, Guadalupe, the wife of Cayetano, some other people, and I took the *little things.* This time I saw strange beings. They appeared to be people but they weren't familiar; they didn't even appear to be fellow Mazatecs.

"I don't know what's happening. I see strange people," I told Guadalupe.

I asked her to pray because I felt a certain uneasiness at that vision. Guadalupe prayed to help me. She prayed to God the Christ.

I received the explanation of that vision I had in a few days when Cayetano arrived at my house in the course of the morning. His words didn't fail to astonish me:

"María Sabina," he said, still breathing hard from the walk, "some blonde men have arrived at the Municipal Building to see me. They've come from a faraway place with the aim of finding a Wise One. They come in search of *Little-One-Who-Springs-Forth*. I don't know whether it displeases you to know it, but I promised to bring them to meet you. I told them that I knew a true Wise Woman. The thing is that one of them, looking very serious, put his head up close to my ear and said: 'I'm looking for *ʔntixitjo.*'[11] I couldn't believe what I was hearing. For a moment I doubted it, but the blonde man appeared to know a lot about the matter. That was the impression I got. The man seems sincere and good. Finally I promised to bring them to your house."

"If you want to, I can't say no. You are an official and we are friends," I replied.

The following day, somebody brought three blonde men to my house. One of them was Mr. Wasson. I told the foreigners that I was sick though not precisely that a drunk had wounded me with a pistol. One of the visitors listened to my chest. He put his head on my chest to hear my heartbeat, held my temples between his hands, and put his head against my back. The man nodded while he touched me. Finally he said some words that I didn't understand; they spoke another language that wasn't Castilian. I don't even understand Castilian.

---

11. [TRANSLATOR'S NOTE] In the transcription of Mazatec words, here as elsewhere, the *x* is pronounced *sh* in English, the modified question mark is a glottal stop (as noted earlier), and the *j* is the Spanish *jota* pronounced like the English *h*. Superinscribed numbers used in more technical transliterations to indicate tones have been omitted throughout in order to make the words more accessible to non-Mazatec readers.

One night soon after, the foreigners witnessed my vigil. Afterward I found out that Wasson had been left marveling, and that he went so far as to say that another person in Huautla who claimed to be a Wise One was nothing but a liar. In reality he meant the sorcerer Vanegas.

When the foreigners took the *saint children* with me, I didn't feel anything bad. The vigil was fine. I had different visions than usual. I saw places I had never imagined existed. I reached the place of origin of the foreigners. I saw cities. Big cities. Many houses, big ones.

Wasson came other times. He brought his wife and his daughter. Different people came with him as well.

One day Wasson arrived with a group of people. Among them were some fellow Mazatecs who brought a sick person wrapped up in a mat. They told me that he was an orphan, Perfecto by name, and that he had been raised by Aurelio-Path. This Aurelio was a Wise One as well, and he had tried to cure the sick boy.

But there was no remedy for the sick one. His death was near. After I saw Perfecto's appearance, I said to Aurelio, "This child is in a very grave condition. He requires a lot of care."

I took the *children* and began to work. In the trance I found out that Perfecto's spirit had been frightened. His spirit had been trapped by a malevolent being.

I let myself be carried away by the Language that sprang from me, and though Perfecto didn't take the *little mushrooms,* my words made him get up and succeed in standing. He related, then, that while resting in the shade of some coffee trees in Cañada Mamey he "felt something" in back of him.

"I had the feeling that there was something behind me," he said, "like an animal, like a donkey. I heard him lick his chops very clearly. I turned around rapidly, but I didn't see anything. That frightened me a lot and since then I've felt sick. It's true, Papa Aurelio, if you take care of me, I'll get well. María Sabina says so."

In the course of the vigil, the sick one got to his feet because the Language gave him strength. I also rubbed some San Pedro on his arms.

Weeks went by and somebody informed me that Perfecto had died. They didn't take care of him as they should have. If they had done several vigils he would certainly have gotten well. They didn't do it.

Wasson, his family and friends went and didn't come back anymore. It's been years since I've seen them; but I know that his wife died. Only Wasson returned once not many years ago. The last time I saw him he told me: "María Sabina, you and I will still live for many years."

After those first visits of Wasson, many foreign people came to ask me to do vigils for them. I asked them if they were sick, but they said no ... that they had only come "to know God." They brought innumerable objects with which they took what they call photographs and recorded my voice. Later they brought papers [newspapers and magazines] in which I appeared. I've kept some papers I'm in. I keep them even though I don't know what they say about me.

It's true that Wasson and his friends were the first foreigners who came to our town in search of the *saint children* and that they didn't take them because they suffered from any illness. Their reason was that they came to find God.

Before Wasson nobody took the mushrooms only to find God. The little mushrooms were always taken for the sick to get well.

15

I've belonged to the sisterhoods for thirty years. Now I belong to the Sisterhood of the Sacred Heart of Jesus. The sisterhood is composed of ten women. If the society is composed of men it is called a *mayordomía* (stewardhood). Each member is also called mother. Our task consists of making candles and gathering money to pay for the mass that is given monthly in thanks to the Sacred Heart of Jesus. Each member gives the principal mother fifty centavos. Between all of us we get together five pesos; but if the mass is for the day of the festival of the Sacred Heart, or some other saint, then we give three pesos. We get together a total of thirty pesos. We give three pesos for the day of the Virgin of the Nativity which is the eighth of September; we also give three pesos the third Friday in March—those are our festival days. In Holy Week, when our Father is crucified, we give three pesos as well.

The priest has a list on which the name and contribution of each member is noted. The Bishop is also aware of it.

Fifteen days before the Festival of the Patron, the stewards and the members of the sisterhood go for a crucifix lent by the church. The principal steward carries the crucifix in his hand.

With flowers donated by the members of the sisterhood, an altar is decorated in the house of the principal steward; and in the path to the house, an arch of bamboo is made, adorned with flowers. The committee that went for the crucifix is received beneath the arch. Rockets are fired and flowers are strewn in the path of the crucifix. The committee of mothers and stewards is accompanied by music. The mothers go along incensing the crucifix committee with copal, and each one carries candles and flowers. At the head of the procession, a steward goes along ringing a bell.

Upon arriving at the house of the principal steward, each member of the sisterhood should hand in a pound of pure wax. Each pound of wax is melted and worked in the presence of the crucifix. The candles that are made are adorned with paper and a bow the same color as the patron saint's clothing. After the wax has been worked, the members of the sisterhood give three pesos each to pay for the mass. This is a festival day. The musicians play and people drink *aguardiente,* smoke, and fire rockets. The candles are blessed in that way. Those candles are sacred from then on and shouldn't be lit except in religious ceremonies. They are not for giving light in the dark.

The day before the fiesta, the stewards go to neighbors' houses to ask for monetary aid. After noon the musicians arrive at the house of the principal mother. There *aguardiente* is drunk and cigarettes are passed out. A goat is killed and eaten in a stew together with bitter tamales. The stewards arrive with their wives, each of whom brings thirteen candles of a half pound each. The members of the sisterhood bring flowers of all kinds.

The musicians play the *Orange Flower,* and then the principal mother dances with the principal steward. The second mother dances with the second steward, the third mother dances with the third steward.

In the evening, the mothers and stewards take the thirteen candles to the church to light them at the altar of the patron saint, while the priest says the rosary.

The next morning, on the festival day of the patron, the stewards and the mothers leave the house of the principal steward and in procession head for the church to hear the mass in which the candles are lighted again, held by the mothers in their hands. Once the mass is over, the candles are put out and the mothers take them with them. The mothers and the stewards gather again in the house of the principal steward where music is played on guitars and the *salterio* [plucked dulcimer]. There stew is again eaten together with bitter tamales, and people smoke and dance. The stewards and some of the mothers drink *aguardiente*.

When the festival is finished, the stewards go to the Municipal Building and return the money to the authorities that they borrowed at the start for the expenses of the festival.

Every two, four, or six years, the members of the sisterhood rotate, so that each one is the principal mother once.

One never ceases to be a mother. When one dies, the sacred candles that are her property and that were not used are put in the coffin next to the corpse.

It is nearly thirty years since I learned of the sisterhoods. It came from the church, I think. From the start I participated in the sisterhoods with enthusiasm because I've always had respect for everything that has to do with God. I obey the priests. I am also obedient to the words of the municipal authorities. They are the heads. They govern us.

When the sisterhoods were begun, thirty years ago, I met Apolonio Terán in church. The two of us, as a couple, went to the houses of the neighbors to invite them to form the first sisterhood and the first mayordomía. I knew that Apolonio was a great Wise Man, that he had the power to cure. That he knew how to speak with the Lords of the Mountains. The two Wise Ones, he and I, joined together in this task without ever speaking of our own wisdom. We only spoke about questions pertaining to the sisterhoods and mayordomías. At that time I didn't make myself known. The wise shouldn't go around advertising what they are, because it is a delicate matter. Apolonio was an active man, he formed the sisterhoods and the mayordomías. He gave people's names to the municipal authorities who took it upon themselves to communicate, in writing, with the elected people. The written paper was the nomination that was given to people who were asked to appear on a certain day. Once the society was formed, the authorities themselves lent money to begin the activities of the mothers and the stewards. The money was used to buy the wax with which the candles are made. Later the borrowed money was returned.

Apolonio and I considered the opinion of the husband, the parents, the brothers and sisters, or the children of the person who was going to become a member of the sisterhood or the mayordomía.

16

I have suffered. And I go on suffering. Here, below the right hip, in the place where I was hit by the bullet the drunk shot at me, a tumor has come out. It has grown little by little and hurts me if it's cold. It will be five years since some people from the city came and wanted to take me there. They said that Wise-Ones-In-Medicine from those parts would cut out the tumor. Before deciding, I consulted the municipal president, Valeriano García; he opposed my going to Mexico City for them to cure me.

"You might die in the moment that they are cutting out the tumor," he said. "We could be left without María Sabina, and that would make us very sad."

Since I obey the authorities, I refused to accompany those people.

I have suffered from poverty. My hands became callous from hard work. My feet are covered with calluses as well. I've never used shoes but I know the paths. The muddy, dusty, rocky paths have made the soles of my feet hard.

Never has evil come from me, nor lies either. I have always been poor: poor I have lived and poor I will die. I have suffered. My two husbands died. Several of my children died from sickness or in tragedies. Some children died when they were very small; others were born without life. I didn't cure the little ones with my power, because at that time I had a husband: relations with men invalidate the power of the *children.*

There has been sadness in my heart. I have had to raise some of my orphaned grandchildren. One of my grandsons died recently with a swollen face. He worked as a laborer opening roads where the metal contraptions go but he drank a lot of *aguardiente,* poor thing, he was hardly twenty years old. Now I'm raising another little one. I like children. I like to caress them and talk with them. . . . It's necessary to take good care of children. They should be baptized as soon as they're born, because children who aren't baptized die if a storm occurs. The lightning bolts of the storm carry away the spirit of the children who haven't been baptized. Just last night I heard the noise produced by a lightning bolt that fell nearby here, and today they notified me that a baby had died in the house of a neighbor.

Catarino, Viviana, and Apolonia, the children of my first husband, are alive and each of them has children. They've withdrawn from me. Family tasks keep them busy, surely. Of my second husband, only my daughter Aurora is alive.

One of my sons, the brother of Aurora, named Aurelio, was murdered. Before the tragedy happened, the *saint children* warned me of it. Those were the days when Wasson came to Huautla. It was a Thursday, during a vigil, when I had a vision: a spotted cattle skin appeared, stretched on the ground to the right of where I was kneeling. I stopped talking once I saw it, but I wasn't intimidated despite the fact that it was a putrid animal hide. It stunk. Afterward a man appeared near the skin, dressed like a fellow Mazatec, and he shouted:

"I'm the one. I'm the one. With this one it will be five. With this one it will be five I've murdered."

A neighbor named Augustín had taken the mushrooms with me to cure himself of pains he felt in the waist. I turned to him to ask:

"Did you see that man? Did you hear what he said?" Augustín answered:

"Yes, I saw him. He's the son of Señora Dolores."

I remained very puzzled; I didn't understand the words of the man who had appeared in my vision. The following day I went on thinking about it without finding an explanation.

My son Aurelio was in Teotitlán del Camino Thursday night.

Three days after having seen the spotted skin, precisely Sunday at noon, three men arrived at my little store; one of them asked for my nineteen-year-old son Aurelio. My son had just arrived from Teotitlán and was in the next room playing the guitar that he had recently bought. One of the men, the son of the neighbor, Dolores, was the same one who had appeared in my vision the Thursday before. My son Aurelio invited them in to where he was and offered them *aguardiente*.

Later the visitors and my son, under the effect of the *aguardiente*, sang, accompanying themselves with the guitar.

After they had sung several songs, there was a brief pause, and suddenly the son of Dolores insulted my son. When I looked in I saw that man lift up his shirt and take a knife out of his belt which he immediately stuck in my son's throat.

I shouted desperately, seeing Aurelio fall on all fours near the doorway to the store.

The killer, taking his knife, fled up the path in the direction of San Miguel, followed by his companions.

I threw myself, crazed from pain and anguish, onto the bloody body of my son, while another of my sons and some friends went off in pursuit of the killer whom they didn't succeed in catching.

My poor Aurelio died right there where he fell. The following day we buried him. The neighbors came to the wake. They drank *aguardiente* and played cards. I gave them coffee, bread, and cigarettes. They put money next to the corpse; with that I paid the expenses of the funeral. We buried him with music as the custom is.

As my son was being buried, I remembered the horrible vision of that previous Thursday. Then I understood what the *little things* had tried to warn me about: the skin, the son of Dolores shouting: "With this one it will be five...." They were warnings of the pain that was approaching.

The men who murdered my Aurelio are now all dead as well. They were bad people. The violence with which they acted turned against them. One by one they were murdered by people who could defend their lives in time. They must have had their reason for murdering my son. I never found out what it was. My Aurelio drank *aguardiente* but he wasn't a violent man. For several months I cried over the death of my son.

And even though I'm the clean woman, the principal clown woman, evil has been done to me. Once they burned my house of seven arm-lengths. It was built of wood with a thatched roof of dried sugarcane leaves. I don't know the reason why they did it. Some people thought it was because I had revealed the ancestral secret of our native medicine to foreigners.

It's true that before Wasson nobody spoke so openly about the *children*. No Mazatec revealed what he knew about this matter. But I obeyed the *síndico;* nevertheless, I think now that if the foreigners had arrived without any recommendation, I would still have shown them my wisdom, because there is nothing bad in that. The *children* are the blood of Christ. When we Mazatecs speak of the vigils we do it in a low voice, and in order not to pronounce the name that they have in Mazatec (*?ntixitjo*) we call them *little things* or *little saints.* That is what our ancestors called them.

Other people believed that the motive for burning my house was that the arsonist thought he was bewitched by me. I've already said, I'm not a Sorceress. I'm a Wise Woman. Still others said that it was the envy malevolent people felt for my power. I never found out the true motive that impelled them to do me harm. I don't even know the name of the arsonist, because I wasn't interested in consulting the *little things* about it.

Along with the house, my little store burned together with the corn, beer, *aguardiente,* the toasted seeds, and cigarettes I sold, my huipils and shawls.... Christ! Everything. That day I wasn't at home. It was empty. My children and I had gone to San Miguel to the fiesta of Saint Michael to sell bread and candles. Upon returning we found nothing but ashes. Without knowing who to turn to, I went into the woods with my children. We ate wild tubers to subsist. In order not to feel so cold we made tea from lemon and orange leaves. Doña Rosaura García, a neighbor in Huautla whom I met in one of the visits of Mr. Wasson, gave me a metal cup. Another person, I don't remember who, gave me a gourd bowl. That was of use to me.

Finally we went to live in the house of some relatives. And it was necessary to begin anew. I worked a lot to build another house. This one of adobe with a corrugated iron roof and I live in it to this day.

But not all has been suffering. I become content listening to music on the salterio. I like music. The Principal Ones like it too. Now I remember that when they gave me the Book, there was music. The drum sounded, the trumpet, the violin, and the salterio. It's because of that I sing:

> I am the drummer woman
> I am the trumpet woman
> I am the woman violinist ...

I even had a salterio myself. I bought it and kept it in my house. I bought it because in a vigil the children asked me: "Do you have a salterio?" and I said, "No, no, I don't have one." After I bought my salterio I answered them, "Yes, yes, I have a salterio."

Those who knew how to play the salterio came to my house to play it. At times I lent it, but one day suffering from lack of money, I sold it. Now I know that the salterio is in Santa Cruz de Juárez.

And I like to dance the Mazatec *jarabe*. I dance it in my visions with the Principal Ones. A Principal One is my partner. Afterward we drink beer and we talk. But I also dance at the festivals of the stewards. On one occasion I danced for the young Wise Man (Dr. Guerra) the *Orange Flower,* the Mazatec *jarabe,* in the house of Doña Rosaura García, for them to see that I'm a woman who likes to enjoy herself. But I don't only dance, I also cook. Once I prepared edible mushrooms for the foreigners. I think that it was in the house of the teacher Herlinda Martínez. In a big pot we cooked *tjaincoa* (white mushrooms), those that grow on balsa trees. We made a hot *tezmole* seasoned with onions. The foreigners ate until their stomachs were full.

1 7

The blonde people, men and women, arrive at my door. They call me "grandma" or "Sabinita" from outside, so I go out and invite them in.

To those who would like some, I give coffee; I don't have anything more to offer them. I think that some of the blonde ones feel good in my house, as if it was theirs, because they spread their blankets or mats on the ground and rest there. At this time of year the foreigners visit me, but not all of them want vigils; they come as well in the dry season, when the *children* don't grow. The foreigners take photographs of me wherever I happen to be. They take photographs of me going along the path with my load of corn on my back or resting on a rock in the marketplace. I've become accustomed to all that. That reminds me that somewhere in Oaxaca City, there's an enormous photograph of me working the earth with a hoe. The people who took that picture of me bought my hoe and took it with them. I like people to give me photographs of myself.

A lot of people come to visit me. Some say they are lawyers, others say they have important posts in the city; they take my picture with their objects, standing next to me themselves, and give me some coins when they go. The people who make papers come; they bring their Mazatec interpreters and ask questions about my life. I'm sorry I don't know Castilian or how to write; otherwise, I myself would say what I know in the papers.

I know that Mr. Wasson has made records and books of my Language.

Some years ago, I was in Tehuacán for a month. Herlinda, a teacher here in Huautla, accompanied me. My stay in Tehuacán was to correct the translation that two foreign missionaries—named Florencia and George—had made of my Language. These missionaries spoke our Mazatec language well, but I couldn't know if they exactly understood my Language. If I could read what they wrote, I would know. I realized that they had some difficulty understanding me.

With the priest, Alfonso Aragón, who was in Huautla for many years, I had a great friendship. This priest had a record on which my Language was recorded; I found that out one day when he invited me to listen to it. He told me that that record was worth a lot, that it was priceless. I thanked him for his words. I had that record myself. I imagine that it was Wasson himself who sent it to me so that I could listen to it. He also gave me a record player. But some people came from the city who said they were officials and took everything.

In the rainy season, when the *little saints* grow in our damp earth, more foreigners come to my house. They continue to seek me but I don't give vigils for them any longer, because I'm too old. My body gets weaker every day; I breathe with difficulty, I don't go down to the market in Huautla very often because I get very tired. There are times when my body is so weak that I fall down on the path or inside the house. I slip easily on the trails; I can't lift the axe any longer with which I used to split kindling.

Now, when I get together some money, I buy kindling and sell it to the neighbors. My biggest dream these last years has been to have a little store where I could once again sell soap, cigarettes, and soda to the passersby; but I've never had sufficient money.

More or less seven years ago, a Bishop came who wanted to take the *saint children*. I would have given them to the Bishop because I know that Bishops are great too, but it wasn't the season. It was March, and the *children* grow in June, July, August, and September, although in some cold zones they can be found during November and December, but they can only rarely be obtained in April or March. If I have a patient in the season when the mushrooms can't be found, I resort to the Leaves of the Shepherdess. Ground up and taken, they work like the *children*. Of course the Shepherdess doesn't have as much strength. Other plants exist called Seeds of the Virgin. These seeds were created by the Virgin. I don't use the seeds, although some Wise Ones do.

The Bishop advised me to initiate my children into the Wisdom I have. I told him that the color of the skin or the eyes can be inherited, including the manner of crying or of smiling, but the same can't be done with wisdom. Wisdom can't be inherited. Wisdom is brought with one from birth. My wisdom can't be taught; that's why I say that nobody taught me my Language, because it is the Language the *saint children* speak upon entering my body. Whoever isn't born to be wise can't attain the Language although they do many vigils. Who could teach a Language like that? My daughter Apolonia just helps me to pray or to repeat my Language during the vigils. She speaks and says what I ask her to, but she isn't a Wise Woman; she wasn't born with that destiny. Apolonia is devoted to raising her children and attending to her husband. She has grown children who live in Mexico City; they work there and send some money to their mother. Apolonia and Viviana, my two daughters, will never be Wise Women. They will not receive the Book from the hands of the Principal Ones. I, on the other hand, am known in Heaven, and even the holy Pope knows I exist. Important people know that I have been born. In the vigils I hear them say that I am the little aquatic Woman of the Book, that I am the Woman of the Flowing Water. It's true, that's why I'm humble, but I'm also "the woman who ascends."

Not anyone can be wise. I make that clear to people. One day I got angry with a school teacher. I got angry with her because she didn't want to give me some money that she should have given me. She assured me that she didn't have any money for me. I told her:

"You're a teacher and supposedly you teach children, but you want to make fun of me; you think you're superior because you know how to read and write. You should know that I don't feel insignificant before anyone. You know how to read and write thanks to the fact that your parents sent you to school to learn. You had to go to school many days to know what you know; but you should understand that I didn't have to go to any school to be wise. We Wise Ones don't need to learn what we know in a school. Wisdom comes from birth. It comes together with one when one is being born—like the placenta."

The mushrooms have revealed to me how I was in the days when I was in the womb of my mother: it's a vision in which I see myself turned into a fetus. An illuminated fetus. And I know that at the moment I was born, the Principal Ones were present. Also the heart of Christ was there.

The foreigners brought me a foreigner with a big fat body. He looked stupid. He didn't say a word. I did a vigil because those people who accompanied him wanted to see if the children could cure the sick in the city where they live. The vigil was done in the house of Cayetano García.

The reaction of the stupid foreigner was that, past midnight, he roared like a lion. Ay! it frightened me for a moment, but the Language gave me courage. When Guadalupe, Cayetano's wife, heard the roar, she took her newborn baby away. She got it out of there so that the foreigner who roared wouldn't catch the little baby's spirit. It sometimes happens that if the "luck" of a person goes out, that "luck," on becoming free, can enter into the body of another person nearby. One gets better and the other gets sick. The man who roared could have transferred his "luck" to the recently born baby. The stupid foreigner went back to his country, and I don't know what's become of him since.

On a more recent occasion, a foreign couple asked me to give them the *little things* because they had a five-year-old son who was suffering from pimples on his head. The mother of the child and I both took the *children*. In the course of the vigil, the child began to cry. He cried a lot. Then it was revealed to me that the mother of the child was herself the cause of the child's sickness. Christ! It scared me to be near that lady, but I armed myself with courage and took a hold of her hair:

"Give me the spirit of the child," I told her in Mazatec. "Give it to me, give it to me," I repeated, shouting in the lady's ears while I pulled hard on her hair.

Little by little the child stopped crying as the lady gave me back his spirit. The truth was that she had a malevolent being inside her who had enchanted the spirit of her own son.

At dawn the couple took their child. They said that they were grateful for the cure. Although the pimples hadn't disappeared from the child's head, his appearance was better now than the day before the vigil. The lady said good-bye to me nicely ... but she never knew that she herself had trapped her son's spirit, causing the pimples on his head.

1 8

For a time there came young people of one and the other sex, long-haired, with strange clothes. They wore shirts of many colors and used necklaces. A lot came. Some of these young people sought me out for me to stay up with the *Little-One-Who-Springs-Forth*. "We come in search of God," they said. It was difficult for me to explain to them that the vigils weren't done from the simple desire to find God, but were done with the sole purpose of curing the sicknesses that our people suffer from.

Later I found out that the young people with long hair didn't need me to eat the *little things*. Fellow Mazatecs weren't lacking who, to get a few centavos for food, sold the *saint children* to the young people. In their turn, the young people ate them wherever they liked: it was the same to them if they chewed them up seated in the shade of coffee trees or on a cliff along some trail in the woods.

These young people, blonde and dark-skinned, didn't respect our customs. Never, as far as I remember, were the *saint children* eaten with such a lack of respect. For me it is not fun to do vigils. Whoever does it simply to feel the effects can go crazy and stay that way temporarily. Our ancestors always took the *saint children* at a vigil presided over by a Wise One.

The improper use that the young people made of the *little things* was scandalous. They obliged the authorities in Oaxaca City to intervene in Huautla ... though not all the foreigners are bad, it's true. In those days, some people arrived at my house who spoke Castilian and dressed like people from the city. A Mazatec interpreter came with them.

They entered my house without my inviting them in. Their eyes fell on some *saint children* that I had on a little table. Pointing at them, one of them asked:

"If I asked you for mushrooms, would you give them to me?"

"Yes, because I believe you've come in search of God," I told him.

Another one, with an authoritarian voice, ordered me:

"You're coming with us to San Andrés Hidalgo. We're going there in search of another person who, like you, dedicates himself to making people crazy."

Meanwhile the other people who came in the group searched my house everywhere. One of them pointed out to the rest of them a bottle that contained San Pedro. I said to them decisively:

"It's ground tobacco mixed with lime and garlic. We call it San Pedro. It serves as a protection against evil spirits."

"Is it smoked?" asked one of the men in a loud voice.

"No," I replied. "It's a tobacco that's rubbed on the arms of the sick, and a little can also be placed inside the mouth.... Our ancestors used it and they called it San Pedro. San Pedro has a lot of force. It helps to get rid of sickness."

Another one of them brought the papers that spoke about me. He also showed the others the record and the record player that Wasson had given me. They all turned around to look at me, and I said to myself: "I can't talk Castilian with them, but they can see in those papers who I am." Afterwards, with a touch of gentleness, they helped me up into a truck. I obeyed without offering resistance. I sat between the man who drove and another one who sat next to the door. That second one continued leafing through the papers in which photographs of me appeared. I realized that from time to time he looked at me out of the corner of his eye.

At no time did fear seize me although I understood that these people were authorities and were trying to do me harm. We arrived at San Andrés and there they arrested the municipal agent. Finally I found out that they accused this man and me of selling a tobacco that drove the young people crazy.

Afterward they took us to the town president's office. A doctor from the Instituto Indigenista spoke with the men. They talked a long while. At the end the doctor told me:

"Don't worry, María Sabina, nothing will happen to you. We're here to defend you."

The men who arrested me also said:

"Forgive us. Go home and rest."

But they took my San Pedro tobacco, the papers, my record, and the object that made it sound. They set the municipal agent of San Andrés at liberty too.

Genaro Terán was the municipal president of Huautla. He told me that a fellow Mazatec, whom the police were after originally, had accused me of selling the young people a tobacco that drove them crazy when they smoked it. The president revealed to me the name of my accuser.

"President," I said to Genaro Terán, "you know that our people don't use the tobacco that this unfortunate claims I sell. They accuse me of bringing gringos to my house. It's the gringos who come in search of me. They take photographs of me, they talk with me, they ask me questions, the same I've answered many times before, and they go after taking part in a vigil. None of these young people has gone crazy in my house. But what is this all about? What harm have I done to this man who accuses me? In all my life I've never had anything to do with him. I know him, he's the son of the late Josefina, our fellow townswoman, but I've never done any harm to this individual. This situation makes me mad. I'm ready to get into a fistfight with the man. And if he wants to fight with a knife, I have mine. And if he wants to fight with a pistol, I'll see how I can get a hold of one. If afterward the judge sentences me to several years in jail, it won't matter in the least. I'll have sated my fury. I don't like people to make fun of me."

"Don't worry," said Genaro Terán, "the case has been settled. You aren't guilty of anything. Go home, María Sabina."

It was an infamy. In vain the man wears pants. His lie hurt me. That's why I was ready to go to jail or die to prove I wasn't guilty. That man, maybe to get some money, sold the *saint children* and the tobacco that drove the young people crazy.

Finally the authorities took that man to jail because his guilt was proven.

The Huautla authorities explained to me that some foreigners were bad, that they came to spoil our customs. . . .

Two years later, Señor Felícitos Pineda, the new municipal president, sent me an official paper in which I was asked to present myself before the public attorney in Teotitlán del Camino. It was then, Álvaro, that you took me to Mexico City. I lived in the house of some of your relatives. And you took me to a man who writes in the papers and who, like so many others, asked me questions in order to later ask the authorities to leave me in peace. Also you took me to a very big house where there were objects made by our ancestors, stones that indigenous hands carved hundreds of years ago. There were photographs of Mazatecs there. What I liked the most was to listen to my voice there, sounding incessantly. My wise Language in that place—I could hardly believe it. I remember people came up to me to greet me. They recognized me. I also remember a picture on the wall in which I seemed to see malignant beings. Beings with black wings. I think that the demons are like that, but we Mazatecs don't have an image of the devil; for us he doesn't have a face or form.

When I returned to Huautla, Felícitos Pineda insisted that I should go before the Principal Ones in Oaxaca because they kept demanding that I appear. A few days later I presented myself in that city. I was accompanied by one of the municipal authorities of Huautla, who explained to me that he would take me to a person, a Principal of great authority in Oaxaca. With courage, without fear of anything, I let myself be conducted to the appointed place. The moment the person saw me, he shouted my name and stood up. Smiling, he came up to me. His attitude was the contrary of what I expected. He embraced me, caressed my hair, and said:

"I wanted you to come to tell you that there is nothing against you."

We talked a moment. On taking leave of him I thanked the person for his words and right away returned to Huautla.

Now I have gone to the city on various occasions. In the first week of July, the municipal authorities of Huautla themselves take me to the *Guelaguetza* festival in Oaxaca. I put on my best huipil and sit there next to the Principal Ones. The nuns who are established in Huautla once took me to Mexico City, and I went with them to various churches. Among them we visited the Shrine where our Virgin Guadalupe is.

1 9

During the vigil, the candles of beeswax that are used in the vigils should be put out; the darkness serves as a background for the images that one is seeing. It isn't necessary to close one's eyes, it's enough to look toward the infinite background of the darkness. There the Principal Ones appear seated around the table on which are all the things of this world. The table displays the clock, the eagle, and the opossum....

There are different classes of *children:* those that grow in the detritus of sugarcane; those that grow in cattle excrement (called San Isidro); those that grow on rotten trees (called "birds"); and those that grow in the damp ground (called "landslide"). Those of the sugarcane and the "landslide" varieties are stronger than the "birds" and San Isidro.

The day that I did a vigil for the first time in front of foreigners, I didn't think anything bad would happen, since the order to give a vigil for the blonde ones came directly from the municipal authorities at the recommendation of the *síndico,* my friend Cayetano García. But what was the result? Well, that many people have come in search of God, people of all colors and all ages. The young people are the ones who have been the most disrespectful. They take the *children* at any time and in any place. They don't do it during the night or under the direction of the Wise Ones, and they don't use them to cure any sickness either.

But from the moment the foreigners arrived to search for God, the *saint children* lost their purity. They lost their force; they spoiled them. From now on they won't be of any use. There's no remedy for it.

Before Wasson, I felt that the *saint children* elevated me. I don't feel like that anymore. The force has diminished. If Cayetano hadn't brought the foreigners ... the *saint children* would have kept their power. Many years ago when I was a child, they grew everywhere. They grew around the house; those weren't used in the vigils, because if human eyes see them they invalidate their purity and strength. One had to go to distant places to search for them, where they were out of reach of human sight. The person who was going to gather them had to observe four days before of sexual abstinence. During those four days it was prohibited to attend wakes in order to avoid the contaminated air of the dead.

The air that surrounds a corpse is impure; if people have wounds and get near a wake, they can get gangrene. Another recommendation to the person sent to gather the *saint children* was that, preferably, he or she should do it after taking a bath. These last few years, anyone looks at the *children,* and no care is taken in gathering them.

The corpses of animals also produce gangrene. Anything decomposed is impure.

Some foreigners say that they come to cure themselves, and there's no lack of those who assure you that they've had operations without being cured. After they've participated in a vigil with me, they thank me and say they feel better. They say they have sugar in their blood. I don't know that sickness. I only know that the spirit is what gets sick. And the spirit is what enriches: people who have made a fortune are ones whose spirits have journeyed to the spiritual realm of wealth. This is a place where there is fortune, greatness, and happiness. The spirit arrives in this realm and robs what it can. If it succeeds in grabbing some wealth, the person will come to have money or will attain important posts. But the spirit should be careful not to be surprised by the watchmen of the realm of wealth. If a watchman surprises a spirit robbing wealth, he wounds him with a pistol. That's how spirits receive the impact of a bullet. The spirit travels and the person dreams it.

To cure people who have fever, I sacrifice a chick, opening its breast with the thumbs of my hands. I extract the heart and I give it, still beating, to the sick person to eat. The chick's corpse can be left in the highest part of a bush; that way it doesn't rot, it just dries out.

But I am old and sick. It's true, life ends. And not only do I try to cure the illnesses of some foreigners, but they have also tried to cure my afflictions. They give me medicines, or people who say they are wise ones in medicine from the city visit me and want to cut out my tumor. I don't pay much attention to them. But there's always one thing that stops me from taking the medicines or allowing them to cut out the tumor. The truth is that I don't want to take the foreigners' medicine because I have my own damp medicine. One day a doctor probed my body and left medicines for me to take, but I didn't do it because at that time many children were dying here in my section of town. The cause of those deaths was that the elves, the masters of the places where they opened the road that goes to San Miguel and that passes near my house, charged for the profanation done to them in ruining the quietness of their places by taking many children. I didn't take the medicines because the sickness of a person who is taking medicine can get worse if at the same time she goes to a wake or there is a dead person next door. Those who know that my back hurts and that it costs me work to swallow give me a massage. First a foreign man and later a woman have given me massages. I think they were experts because afterward I felt relieved from the pains in my body. Not all the foreigners are bad. Some bring me food or fruit and I thank them. As for those who use my hearth to prepare a meal for me, I ask them to pardon me because I don't have spoons. They know that I'm poor and that I live alone except for an orphaned grandson who keeps me company.

The people who arrive at my door always bring me gifts. The governor of Oaxaca, Zárate Aquino, gave me two mattresses. He said that a soft bed gives more comfort to the body than the hard ground where mats are spread. To use the mattresses, I bought two wooden beds.

A young foreigner who wore multicolored clothes and sandals wanted to give me a big, pretty dog. I told him that I didn't want a dog, that I didn't have the money to maintain it. What was the animal going to eat? Shit? The young foreigner understood my situation and took his dog with him.

I like songbirds. Two years ago I bought a chachalaca from Cañada Mamey. I bought it for eighty pesos. I knew that a storm was coming when the chachalaca began to coo; it was like a companion for me but, Jesus Christ, they robbed it from me. Now I don't have a chachalaca to distract me.

20

But I have never seen the demons, although to arrive where I should I pass through the dominions of death. I submerge myself and walk down below. I can search in the shadows and in the silence. Thus I arrive where the sicknesses are crouched. Very far down below. Below the roots and the water, the mud and the rocks. At other times I ascend, very high up, above the mountains and the clouds. Upon arriving where I should, I look at God and at Benito Juárez. There I look at the good people. There everything is known. About everything and everyone, because there everything is clear. I hear voices. They speak to me. It is the voice of *Little-One-Who-Springs-Forth*. The God that lives in them enters my body. I cede my body and my voice to the *saint children*. They are the ones who speak; in the vigils they work in my body and I say:

> Because you gave me your clock
> Because you gave me your thought
> Because I am a clean woman
> Because I am a Cross Star woman
> Because I am a woman who flies
>
> I am the sacred eagle woman, says
> I am the lord eagle woman, says
> I am the lady who swims, says
> Because I can swim in the immense
> Because I can swim in all forms
> Because I am the launch woman
> Because I am the sacred opossum
> Because I am the lord opossum

I can be eagle, opossum, or woman clock. If I see them, I pronounce their names.

The *children* turn into the Principal Ones. The Principal Ones appear as well in the visions of the initiates. On their sacred table, they put clocks, papers, books, communion wafers, stars, dew, or eagles.... The Principal Ones ask the initiates:

"What type of Wise One do you want to be? Do you want the Lords of the Mountains, the masters of the places, to guide you, or do you want God the Christ to guide you?"

Then the initiate chooses and tells the Principal Ones what he or she prefers. At that moment the initiate receives a Book that contains the Language the person has chosen.

I decided for God the Christ. I made it known to the Principal

Ones. The realm of the Principal Ones is the realm of abundance. There, there is beer and music. When I'm in that realm I ask for beers to be served to everyone. A Principal One serves the beer and then all together we give a toast. There are times when it isn't necessary to ask for beers, they're within reach of the hand. If music sounds, I dance as a partner with the Principal Ones; and I also see that words fall, they come from up above, as if they were little luminous objects falling from the sky. The Language falls on the sacred table, falls on my body. Then with my hands I catch word after word. That happens to me when I don't see the Book.... And I sing:

> With the Virgin Magdalene
> With the Virgin Guadalupe
> With Lord Santiago
>
> Because I am the water that looks, says
> Because I am the woman wise in medicine, says
> Because I am the woman herbalist, says
> Because I am the woman of the medicine, says
> Because I am the woman of the breeze, says
> Because I am the woman of the dew, says

If during the vigil the mushrooms order me to suck out the sickness, I apply suction from where I am; it's not necessary for me to put my mouth against the sick part. And my Language says:

> I come with my thirteen hummingbirds
> Because I am the sacred hummingbird, says
> Because I am the Lord hummingbird, says
> Because I bring my clean sucker, says
> Because I bring my healthy sucker, says
> Because I bring my bamboo tube, says
> My bamboo with dew, says
> My fresh bamboo, says

And it's that ...

> I am the woman Book that is beneath the water, says
> I am the woman of the populous town, says
> I am the shepherdess who is beneath the water, says
> I am the woman who shepherds the immense, says
> I am a shepherdess and I come with my shepherd, says
> Because everything has its origin
> And I come going from place to place from the origin ...

If I put tobacco on the arms of a sick one, then I say:

> And I bring my San Pedro
> Only with San Pedro
> Only with San Pedro
> What I work with
> What I appreciate
> What I work with
> What I appreciate
>
> Our Father cumulus cloud
> Our Father Arosio[12]
> My Father! Father of the dew!
> Father cultivator
> Rich Father

The *little saints* tell me that I am the wife of the Lord of all the Mountains. That is why I say:

> I am the Woman of the Flowing Water ...

They tell me that I am the woman of the oceans, that I bring wisdom in my hands. That I am the woman of Saint Peter and of Saint

12. Arosio is an indecipherable word. María Sabina says that it is "the name of a place in the mountains."

Paul. That I am a child-woman but that I can speak with the heroes. At times I cry but when I whistle nobody frightens me.

And it's that in the middle is Language. On this shore, in the middle, and on the other shore is Language. With the mushrooms I see God, then I sing:

Because I am the God Star Woman
The Cross Star Woman
Because I can swim in the immense
Because I am a well-prepared woman
Because I have my healed people
Because I have my healed priest
And I have my healed Bishop
I have my pure Bishop

Because our people are great
Because our people are excellent
Holy Father
Your house is big
Your house is a house of authority
Our Bishop
People of our heart
Good and clean priest
Good and clean Bishop
Good and clean candle
Good and clean nun
Because your Book exists
Your Book that I bring

Then ...

I am the woman of the sacred Sun Stone, says
I am the woman of the lord Sun Stone, says
I am the shooting star woman, says
I am the shooting star woman beneath the water, says

I am the lady doll, says
I am the sacred clown, says
I am the lord clown, says
Because I can swim
Because I can fly
Because I can follow tracks ...

The *saint children* cure; they cure fever, chills, yellow skin, or toothache. They drive the evil spirits out of the body or rescue the spirit trapped by an enchantment from the masters of the springs or mountains. They heal those who have a "luck" because of sorcery. They are taken and later one vomits the malignant spirit.

If I see papers on the rich table of the Principal Ones, I say:

I am the woman who writes ...

Language belongs to the *saint children.* They speak and I have the power to translate. If I say that I am the little woman of the Book, that means that a *Little-One-Who-Springs-Forth* is a woman and that she is the little woman of the Book. In that way, during the vigil, I turn into a mushroom—little woman—of the Book ...

If I am on the aquatic shore, I say:

I am a woman who is standing in the sand ...

Because wisdom comes from the place where the sand is born.

21

I like to smoke cigarettes and to drink a little *aguardiente,* but I never get drunk. I'm already old. I get tired quickly. My back hurts me and my chest when I swallow my food. I don't talk much because my mouth has lost some teeth. I'm ashamed of being toothless, and it makes it difficult for me to eat tough meat. I prefer to drink liquids.

Since quite a while ago, I live alone, my children have gone their separate ways. Each one is devoted to his or her family. I've been left by myself. My children hardly visit me. The foreigners who come to see me distract me and I feel myself kept company by their presence.

My mother, María Concepción, died less than ten years ago. She was ancient. She got sick and I tried to cure her. I did three vigils to give her strength, but she herself realized that her end was near and that there was no remedy.

A little before dying, she said to me:

"Resign yourself, Bi,"—that's what she called me—"I thank you for what you're doing for me, but it's time for me to die. I don't have anything to reproach you for. On the contrary, I'm content with the attentions that you've given me in life. But I feel bad to leave you. What will become of you after my death? I have confidence that God will know how to take care of you ..."

And I'm old too. That's why I ask God to bless me. I always ask for grace each day ... I ask grace for the world and for myself.

I know that soon I'm going to die. But I'm resigned. I will die at the moment God wills. Meanwhile let life follow its course; let us go on living our time in this world that is Christ's. This world of Christians where there is also evil and discord; in this world where people fight for anything.

I know the realm of death because I've arrived there. It is a place where there is no noise, because noise, no matter how slight, is bothersome. In the peace of that realm, I see Benito Juárez.

The day that I die, what our custom dictates will be done. They will twist the neck of a rooster that should die next to my corpse. The spirit of the rooster will accompany my spirit. The rooster will crow four days after I have been buried; then my spirit will wake up and will go forever to the realm of death. During the wake, my family will place jars of water next to my lifeless head. It will be the water that I will have to take with me so that I'm not overcome by thirst while I journey to the realm of death. Inside my coffin, they will put seven gourd seeds, greens, and some balls of the dead [a wild fruit from the Mazatec mountains], all together in a little cloth bag. It will be the food that I will take so that hunger doesn't bother me on the way.

The women who go to my wake will make *tezmole* with the meat of the sacrificed rooster. The *tezmole* will be eaten only by the reciter of prayers and the people who are going to dig my grave. If I have sacred candles left over from my activities as a member of the sisterhood, they will put them next to my corpse. They will dress me in a clean huipil and my best shawl. Between my hands will be placed a palm cross that has been blessed.

We Mazatecs respect the dead. On the Days of the Faithful Dead, in the first days of November, we make offerings of *cempasúchil* flowers placed in arches of bamboo, and we put on the table fruit and food, tamales with pork, coffee and bread.

A group of people form a band of masqueraders. Each one is called a Bulging Navel. They disguise themselves with masks and the clothing of men or women, and go around to the music of violins, guitars, and a loud drum. They visit the houses of the neighbors, singing:

Bulging Navel
Lime fruit
A favor I ask you for
One favor nothing more
Give me a little lemonade

In each house they dance in couples and eat tamales, drink coffee or *aguardiente.*

And it's that the Bulging Navels represent the souls who, it is said, return to eat and to satiate their thirst for the food of this world.

For many years now, the people who want to disguise themselves as Bulging Navels have come to my house. Here they transform themselves. I lend them the hats with their brims an arm's length wide, woven from vines, that my grandchildren make for them. The rest of the year I keep these big hats hanging from the roof of my house.

September 1975–August 1976
Translation from Spanish by Henry Munn

THE CHANTS

THE FOLKWAYS CHANT

This chant was recorded the night of July 21–22, 1956, by V. P. and R. Gordon Wasson in the home of Cayetano García of Huautla de Jiménez, Oaxaca.

I am a woman who shouts, says
I am a woman who whistles, says
I am a woman who thunders, says
I am a woman who plays music, says
I am a spirit woman, says
I am a woman who shouts, says
Ah, our Jesus Christ, says
Ah, our Jesus, says
Our Saint Peter woman, says
Our Saint Peter woman, says
Our Apostle woman, says
Our shooting star woman, says
Our shooting star woman, says
Our whirling woman of colors, says
Our woman of the fields, says
Ah, our Jesus Christ, says
Our woman santo, says
Our woman santo, says

Our woman santa, says
Our woman of light, says
Our woman santo, says
Our spirit woman, says
Ah, our Jesus Christ, says
Our spirit woman, says
Our woman of light, says
I am a spirit woman, says
I am a woman of light, says
I am a woman of the day, says
I am a clean woman, says
I am a lord eagle woman, says
Ah, our Jesus Christ, says
Our respectable woman, says
Our admirable woman, says
Our woman of light, says
Our spirit woman, says
Ah, our Jesus Christ, says
Our woman who takes flight, says
Ah, our Jesus Christ, says
Our diviner woman, says
Our woman bowed down to the ground, says
Ah, our Jesus Christ, says
Our whirling woman of colors, says
Our Jesus Christ, says
She is a clock woman, says
She is a clean woman, says
Ah, Jesus Christ, says
She is a clean woman, says
She is a well-prepared woman, says

She is a clean soul, says
She is a well-prepared soul, says
She is a well-prepared soul, says
She is a well-prepared soul, says
She is a well-prepared soul, says
Ah, Jesus Christ, says
Ah, Jesus, says
Ah, Jesus Christ, says
Ah, Jesus, says
You holy Father, says
You are the santo, says
You are the santa, says
Ah, it is certain and true

    [The expression is hummed rather than spoken out loud.]

You are the santo, says
You are the santa, says
Those that are santo santo, those that are santa, those that are santo santa
    santo santa, they are the ones that are called santo and santa, says
Santo they are called, says
Santa they are called, says

I am a woman born
I am a woman fallen into the world
I am a law woman
I am a woman of thought
I am a woman who gives life
I am a woman who reanimates
I have the heart of Christ, says
I have the heart of the Virgin
I have the heart of Christ

I have the heart of the Father
I have the heart of the Old One
It's that I have the same soul, the same heart as the santo,
    as the santa, says
You, my Mother Shepherdess, says
You, my Father, says
Living Mother, Mother who sways back and forth, says
Mother of sap, Mother of the dew, says
Mother who gave birth to us, Mother who is present, says
Mother of sap, Mother of milk, says
You, Mother of sap, Mother of milk, says
Green Mother, Mother of clarity, says
Budding Mother, Mother of offshoots, says
Green Mother, Mother of clarity, says
Ah, Jesus Christ, says
Ah, Jesus, says
Our Green Father, says
Our Father of clarity, says
Budding Mother, Mother of offshoots, says
Green Mother, Mother of clarity, says
Ah, Jesus Christ, says
Our woman santo, says
Our woman santa, says
Our spirit woman, says
Our woman of light, says
She is a woman of the day, says
Our woman of light, says
She is a woman of the day, says
She is a woman of light, says
She is a spirit woman, says

Ah, Jesus, says

She is a woman of the light, says

She is a woman of the day, says

She is a woman who takes flight, says

I am a woman who looks into the insides of things, says

I am a woman who investigates, says

I am a woman who shouts, says

I am a woman who whistles, says

I am a woman who resounds, says

I am a woman torn up out of the ground, says

I am a woman torn up out of the ground, says

I am a woman wise in medicine, says

I am a woman wise in herbs, says

Ah, Jesus Christ, says

She is a wolf woman, says

I am a woman wise in medicine, says

I am a woman wise in words, says

I am a woman wise in problems, says

I am a hummingbird woman, says

I am a hummingbird woman, says

I am a little colibrí[1] woman, says

I am a little colibrí woman, says

Ah, Jesus Christ, says

I am a clean woman, says

I am a well-prepared woman, says

I am a Saint Peter woman, says

I am a Saint Peter woman, says

1. The common Spanish word *colibrí* appears interchangeably with English "hummingbird" to distinguish two words or variants in the Mazatec, *tontsin* and *ntsica*.

I am an Apostle woman, says

I am an Apostle woman, says

I am a shooting star woman, says

I am a shooting star woman, says

Cayetano

    [He replies, "Yes. Work, work."]

I am a clean woman, says

I am a well-prepared woman, says

I am a woman who looks into the insides of things, says

I am a woman who looks into the insides of things, says

I am a woman who looks into the insides of things, says

I am a woman who looks into the insides of things, says

I am a woman of light, says

I am a woman of light, says

I am a woman of light, says

I am a woman of the day, says

I am a woman who resounds, says

I am a woman wise in medicine, says

I am a woman wise in words, says

I am a Christ woman, says

Ah, Jesus Christ, says

I am a Morning Star woman, says

I am the God Star woman, says

I am the Cross Star woman, says

I am the Moon woman, says

I am a woman wolf, says

Father Jesus Christ, says

I am a woman of heaven, says

I am a woman of heaven, says

Ah, Jesus Christ, says

I am the woman who knows how to swim, says
I am the woman who knows how to swim in the ocean, says
Because I can go to heaven, says
Because I can swim over the water of the ocean, says
Calmly, says
Without mishap, says
With sap, says
With dew, says
I am the woman of the great expanse of the waters, says
I am the woman of the expanse of the divine ocean, says
Because I can go up to heaven, says
Because I can go over the great expanse of the waters, says
Because I can go over the expanse of the divine ocean, says
Calmly, says
Without mishap, says
With sap, says
With dew, says

Santa santa santa santa santa santa santa santa santa santa santa
san santa san santa santa santo
ma mai ma ma ma ma ma ma ma ma ma ma
ma ma ma ma mai
Who are, who are, who are in the house of heaven
Christ
You Father, you Christ
Ki so so so so so sooo so so si
You my Father, you my Father
You old One
Mother Shepherdess
Mother Conception

Mother Patroness
Our Mother Mary of Mercy
You my Mary Conception
You my Mary Patroness
My Mother
All the santos, all the santos that exist
Mother of Mazatlán
Mother of the Sanctuary
You my Mother of Mazatlán
You my Father of the Sanctuary
My Mother of Ixcatlán
Our Virgin of Baby Water
All the Virgins
All the Fathers

Pa pa pai
Ki so so so (Papa Jesus)
You Mother, Mother, Mother who are in the house of heaven
You Mother who are in the house of heaven
In your beautiful world, says
In your fresh world, says
In your world of clarity, says
I am going there, says
I am arriving there, says
Because I have my palms, I have my hands, says
Because I have a tongue, I have a mouth, says
Because I have my palms, says
Because I have my hands, says
Because I have my tongue, says

Because I am speaking poorly and humbly, I speak to you, you are
    the only one, my Mother, to whom I can speak with humility,
    you my Mother who are in the house of heaven, says
My Father who are in the house of heaven, says
I am going there, says
I am arriving there, says
I go there showing my Book, says
I go there showing my tongue and my mouth, says
I go there holding out my palms, my hands, says
I am a Saint Peter woman, says
I am a Saint Peter woman, says
I am an Apostle woman, says
I am a shooting star woman, says

He is the Father, says
He is the santo, says
She is the santa, says
He is the santo
She is the santa
It is certain, says
It is true, says
I look into the insides of things, says
I investigate, says
My clean Book, says
My well-prepared Book, says
My clean quill, says
My well-prepared quill, says
My clean staff, says
My well-prepared staff, says

It is true, says
Father, says
Cayetano García, says
Strong people, says
He is a father, says
She is a mother, says
Jesus, says
Strong people, says
Great people, says
They are respectable people, says
They are admirable people, says
He also lightnings forth, says
He shouts, says
Cayetano García, says
It is certain, says
It is true, says

Santo
Jesus, Jesus, Jesus
You Mother, you Mother, you Mother Shepherdess, says
Our Mother Conception
Our Mother Patroness
Our Mother Magdalene
You, doll Mother of the Rosary, says
And you, Father of the Sanctuary
Our Father
Green Father
Father of clarity
You my Mother of Mazatlán
Jesus Christ

Mother of Cuicatlán
Mother Patroness
Jesus Christ
Mother Conception
You doll Mother Guadalupe of Mexico and Oaxaca
Jesus Christ
Because it is the paper of the judge
It is the Book of the law
It is the Book of government
I know how to speak with the judge
The judge knows me
The government knows me
The law knows me
God knows me
So it is in reality
I am a justice woman
I am a law woman
It is not anything salted, it is not a lie
Jesus Christ

Ah, Jesu Kri
I am a woman who shouts
I am a woman who whistles
I am a woman who lightnings, says
Ah, Jesu Kri
Ah, Jesusi
Ah, Jesusi
Cayetano García
   [She calls his name to get his attention. "Yes," he responds. "Work, work."]
Ah, Jesusi

Woman santa, says

Ah, Jesusi

*[Here she begins humming and clapping, uttering the meaningless syllables
"so" and "si." Throughout the entire passage that follows she goes on clapping
rhythmically in time to her words.]*

hmm hmm hmm

hmm hmm hmm

hmm hmm hmm

hmm hmm hmm

hmm hmm hmm

so so so si

hmm hmm hmm

hmm hmm hmm

Woman who resounds

Woman torn up out of the ground

Woman who resounds

Woman torn up out of the ground

Woman of the principal berries, says

Woman of the sacred berries, says

Ah, Jesusi

Woman who searches, says

Woman who examines by touch, says

ha ha ha

hmm hmm hmm

hmm hmm hmm

She is of one word, of one face, of one spirit, of one light, of one day

hmm hmm hmm

Cayetano García

*[He answers, "Yes …" She says, "Isn't that how?" He responds, "Yes, that's it."
She says, "Isn't that it? Like this. Listen."]*

Woman who resounds
Woman torn up out of the ground
Ah, Jesusi
Ah, Jesusi

   [In the background the man laughs with pleasure.]

Ah, Jesusi
Ah, Jesusi
Ah, Jesusi
hmm hmm hmm
so so so
Justice woman
hmm hmm hmm

   ["Thank you," says the man.]

Saint Peter woman
Saint Paul woman
Ah, Jesusi
Book woman
Book woman
Morning Star woman
Cross Star woman
God Star woman
Ah, Jesusi
Moon woman
Moon woman
Moon woman
hmm hmm hmm
hmm hmm hmm
Sap woman
Dew woman

   [The man urges her on. "Work, work," he says.]

She is a Book woman
Ah, Jesusi
hmm hmm hmm
hmm hmm hmm
so so so
Lord clown woman
Clown woman beneath the ocean
Clown woman
  [The other words are unintelligible.]
Ah, Jesusi
hmm hmm hmm
hmm hmm hmm
so so so
Woman who resounds
Woman torn up out of the ground
hmm hmm hmm
Because she is a Christ woman
Because she is a Christ woman
ha ha ha
so so so
so so so
so so so
Whirling woman of colors
Whirling woman of colors
Big town woman
Big town woman
Lord eagle woman
Lord eagle woman
Clock woman
Clock woman

ha ha ha

so so so

so so so

so so so

    ["That's it. Work, work," exclaims the man.]

hmm hmm hmm

hmm hmm hmm

so so so

hmm hmm hmm

so so so

so so so

si si si

si si si

si si si

so sa sa

si si si

so sa sa sa

hmm hmm hmm

hmm hmm hmm

hmm hmm hmm

si so sooooooooooiiiiii

    [The end of "so" is drawn out into a long tone. She calls, "Cayetano García."
    "Work, work," he replies. She goes on humming, clapping faster and faster.
    "Cayetano García," she calls again, in between her humming, almost as if
    she were animating him, bringing him to himself with her clapping. "Work,
    work," he says, "don't worry." And the passage ends on an expiring "siiiii."]

You my Father

You Christ

You Christ

Along the path of your soles, along the path of your feet

Where you triumphed, Christ
Where your saliva is, where your sweat is, Christ
That is why I am searching for the path of your soles,
    that is why I am searching for the path of your feet
Where you stopped, Christ
Where you stopped, Father
Where you stopped, Old One
You are a respectable Father, an admirable Father
You are a respectable Mother, an admirable Mother
You are a green Father, a Father of clarity
You are a green Mother, a Mother of clarity
You are a budding Mother, a Mother of offshoots
You are a green Mother, a Mother of clarity

Father Jesus Christ
We go to you speaking poorly and humbly, holding out
    our hands to you in supplication
With all of the santos
With all of the santas
Because there are santos, because there are santas
Because there are santos, because there are santas
All the clean spirits
All the good souls
It is a clean soul
It is a well-prepared soul
It is a respectable soul
It is a radiant soul
Greenness and sap
Flower of the dew
Flower in bud

Translucent flower

Flowering flower

Respected flower

Ah, Jesus Christ

It is a flower of fresh water

A flower of clear water

Fresh flower

Translucent flower

Because there are clean flowers where I am going

Because there is clean water where I am going

Clean flower, clean water

Fresh flower

Growing flower

Mine that is increasing

Green mine

Budding mine

There is no wind, there is no spit, there is no garbage, there is no dust

There is no whirlwind, there is no weakness in the air

That is the work of my santos, that is the work of my santas

Ah, Jesus Christ

Ah, Jesusi

Ah, Jesusi

Ah, Jesus Christ

He is the santo

Ah, she is the santa

Ah, he is the santo

Ah, she is the santa

Ah, he is spirit

Ah, he is spirit

Ah, it is light

Ah, it is dew
Ah, it is sap
Ah, it is sap
Ah, it is greenness
Jesus Christ
Jesus
Jesus Christ
There is no resentment, there is no rancor, there is no insult, there is
　　no anger
It is not a matter of insults, it is not a matter of lies
It is a matter of life and well-being, of lifting up, of restoring
　　["Thank you," says the man.]

HERE BEGINS THE SECOND SIDE OF THE RECORD.

You are a man of business, a man of recompense, a man born and
　　fallen into the world, a man of cacao now, you are a man of
　　money, a man with a green staff, a staff of clarity, a respectable
　　man, an admirable man
All the santos
All the santas
Lord Saint Peter
Lord Saint Paul
Peter Scepter
Peter Martyr
With all of the santos, with all of the santas
As many santos as there are
Cayetano García
As many santas as there are
I mention them all

The path of your soles, the path of your feet

Path of sap

Path of dew

Holy Father

In the name of the Son and the Holy Spirit

["Have the people gone to sleep?" she asks Cayetano, meaning Wasson and his
companions. "What?" he says. "Have the people gone to sleep?" "No, they're still
awake." "Ah, they're awake." She then resumes singing in the background, and
Cayetano asks the visitors in Spanish, "You people are still awake, aren't you?"
"Yes, of course," someone answers. "And the other one?" asks Cayetano.]

With all the santas, with all the santas, says

I will prepare as many santos and santas as there are

I will prepare thirteen lord eagles

I will prepare thirteen lord opossums

I will prepare thirteen lord whirlwinds of colors

I will prepare thirteen Saint Peters, Saint Pauls

Peter Scepter

Peter Martyr, says

As the Holy Trinity did and disposed

The path you God the Father followed, the path you God the Son
    followed, the path the Holy Spirit followed

Thus is the path he formed and traced with his clean thought,
    his clean heart

Mountains were formed, ridges were formed

So did he think it out, he examined it, gazing into the heavens and
    into the earth, says

We are looking for the path of your palms, the path of your hands,
    Christ, says

You my Father

With everything in the world

Virgin Mother Shepherdess

Mother of the harvest
Rich Mother
Mother who gives well-being
Green Mother
Powerful Mother
Mother Patroness
Mother Conception
Mother Patroness, says
Jesus
Our doll Virgin Water of the Marketplace
Our doll Virgin under the earth
Woman for whom things multiply, woman for whom things multiply
Woman of paper blackened with smoke, woman of paper blackened
    with smoke, says
Where the Mother was born
Where the Nun was born, says
Where the good and clean Archbishop was born, says
Where the good, clean Father was born, says
Where the clean ocean is, says
Holy Father, says
There we are arriving, says
If there is any evil dream or nightmare, we are going to get rid of it
In the name of the Son and the Holy Spirit
May this sickness of weakness be gotten rid of
Whether it's whirlwind, whether it's wind, says
Whether it's wind, says
Holy Father, says
May the santo come, says
May the santa come, says

May Lord Saint Peter come, says
May Lord Saint Paul come, says
May there come thirteen lord eagles, says
May there come thirteen sacred eagles, says
May there come thirteen lord whirlwinds of colors, thirteen sacred
    whirlwinds of colors, says
May there come thirteen lord big towns, thirteen sacred big towns, says
Because I have my thirteen women who dive beneath the great waters
Because I have my thirteen women who dive into the divine ocean, says
I have my thirteen children scattered beneath the divine ocean, says
Holy Father
With all the santos, with all the santas, says
As did the santo wise in medicine, says
As did the santo wise in herbs, says
Holy Father, says
You turned into medicine, says
You turned into herbs, says
You are the one wise in medicine, says
You are the medic, says
When we are sick you doctor us, says
You treat us with herbs, says
There is no resentment, says
There is no rancor, says
There is no insult, there is no anger, says
The path of business, says
The path of recompense, says
The path of work, says
With all the santos, as many santos and santas as there are
As the Father of the harvest did, rich Father

Father of the harvest, rich Father, says
I supplicated him, I begged him, searching for the medicinal flower,
    searching for the herbal flower

so so so so so sooo
so so so so so so sooo
ki so so so
ma ma ma mai
ma ma mai
ki ki ki ki ki ko kai
ko ka ko ko ko ko ka ki ki ki ki Kristo
siempre siempre *[always, always]*
sien sien sien sien sien siempre
sien sien sien sien siempre
sien sien sien sien sien siempre
ai ai ai
ma ma mai
ki ki ki
ma ma mai
ma ma mai
ki so so soi
I am asking for blessing, for the blessing of life and well-being
What I am asking about is the vine, the root, the offshoots, the buds
Is all the babies and the children
It is for them that I ask blessing
Receive my words, my Mother who are in the house of heaven
Mother Shepherdess
What I ask for is goodness, Mother Shepherdess
You my Mother Shepherdess
Mother of sap, Mother of the dew

Mother of sap, Mother of milk
Mother of the Harvest, rich Mother
Mother who gives well-being, Mother who is present
Christ
You Father Christ
Jesus Christ
Let us go with freshness and clarity
Let us go with light and in the light of day
I think one can live poorly, that one can live humbly, I think one can
    speak, I think one can speak, I think one can dress poorly

Mother of good palms
Mother of good hands
Your words are medicine
Your breath is medicine
That is the work of our flower with sap, our flower of the dew
Our budding children, our sprouting children
Holy Father
You my Father and you Mother who are in heaven
You Christ and you my Father
We are going to doctor, we are going to treat with herbs
That is the work of our budding children, our sprouting children
That is the work of our flower of sap, our flower of the dew
That is the work of the little lord colibrí, the little sacred colibrí
That is the work of our hummingbird children
That is the work of our hummingbird
That is the work of our little colibrí, our little lord colibrí, little
    sacred colibrí
It is the same as the mountain of medicine, the mountain of herbs
Cold herbs, herbs of clarity

Medicinal herbs, sacred herbs
I bring with me thirteen medics beneath the water
I bring with me thirteen medics beneath the ocean
They are children who resound, children torn up out of the ground
Holy Father
You Santo
You Santa
Ah, Jesus Christ
You Santo

   ["Massage her," she tells Cayetano.]
Dew woman, says
Fresh woman
Woman of clarity, says
Woman who prays to heaven
Moon woman
Woman of the day, says
With all the santos, says
With all the santas, says
Holy Father, says
Mother Shepherdess, says
Mother Conception, says
Now that you are in your place and present
Woman of sap, woman of the dew, says
Our doll Mother of the Rosary, says
With all the santos, says
Lord of the Sanctuary, says
Our doll Virgin of Cuicatlán, says
Our doll Virgin of Mazatlán, says
With all the santos
Lord Saint Matthew, says

You who hold the paper in your hands, you who at this moment
    hold the Book in your hands, says
With as many santos, with as many santas as there are santos
With as many santos, as many santas as there are
Now we bow ourselves down before you, speaking with humility
    beneath your shadow, speaking with clarity, says
We speak with tenderness, we speak with clarity, says
We speak with humility, we speak with offshoots, says
We speak with freshness, we speak with clarity, says
Fresh are our words, fresh our breath, fresh our saliva
Words are medicine
Medicine is the breath
Clean saliva, well-prepared saliva, says
Illumination of life, illumination from on high, says
Illumination of the sap, illumination of the dew, says
Holy Father, says
God the Son, says
God the Holy Spirit
Lord Saint Peter
Lord Saint Paul
Peter Scepter
Peter Martyr, says
    [*"Isn't it so?" she asks Cayetano. "It is," he says.*]
Our doll, our Virgin
My Father
Christ
It is your fresh flower, your flower of clarity, my Father
It is your flower of light, your flower of the day, my Father
Your poor flower, your humble flower, my Father
Why are you so poor and humble?

It is not in vain that you bowed down and inclined yourself
We, too, will go on being poor and humble
You, my Father
You, Christ
You, Lord Saint Peter
Our Apostle beneath the water
Our Apostle beneath the ocean
Our Saint Peter
Our Saint Paul
I will go on being poor, my Father
I will go on being humble, Christ
It is your blood that I want you to give me, my Father, your heart is
    what I want you to give me
Give me your words, Christ, your saliva, my Father who are in the
    house of heaven
I will follow the path of your hands, I will follow the path of your feet,
    my Father
Where you stopped, my Father
Where you stopped, Christ
There I am going to leave my Saint Peter woman, my Saint Peter man
Accompany me, Lord Saint Peter, Lord Saint Paul

Mother Patroness
You Heart of Jesus
Jesus Christ
I have your staff of sap, your staff of the dew
I have your good and clean Bishop
I have paper
I have my Book
I am known in the house of heaven

You know me, my Mother

God, my Father, knows me

Jesus Christ, you will always, always reign in the house of heaven

Jesus

Heavenly Mother

I bring your medicinal herbs, your sacred herbs in my palms, in my
    hands

There is no resentment, there is no rancor in what I have in my
    palms, in my hands

It is tenderness and clarity

It is life and well-being

It is buds and sprouts, may they grow, that is what I ask you for,
    Jesus Christ

The path of the years, the path of the days, that is what I ask you for,
    my Father

    ["Thank you," says the man.]

Mother Patroness

Jesus

My Mother Mary

Jesus

I go along the path of your palms, the path of your hands, the path of
    your soles, the path of your feet

I am going there, I am arriving there

There is no resentment, there is no rancor; there is no insult, there is
    no anger; there is no garbage, no dust; there is no whirlwind,
    there is no wind

That is the work of the santo santo santo santo santo santai

That is the work of the santo santa santo santa santo santa santo
    santo santo santo

San santo santo santa santo

Santo santai
Ah, María
Ah, Jesus
Jesus, Jesus
Father
Ma ma ma Mother Mary
Jesus
Jesus Christ, Christ, Mother Mary, Jesus
You, Mother Mary
Santo santo santo santo
I am going to receive there in the path
I am going to receive the enchantment
I am going to receive his light, his day
The path of his soles, the path of his feet
Jesus
Santo santo santo
san san santo
Lord Saint Peter
Lord Saint Paul
Santo santo santo santo
Christ
Mother Shepherdess
Mother Conception
Mother Patroness
Jesus Christ
You Mother Patroness
You Mother Shepherdess
Mother of the harvest, rich Mother
She is a green Mother, a Mother of clarity
Christ

Mother Conception
Mother Patroness
You, Jesus Christ
Mother Shepherdess
Mother Conception
Mother Patroness
Only you, Mother
Santo
You, Christ
You, Holy Child of Atocha
You, Holy Isidro
Father of the harvest, rich Father
He is a green Father, a Father of clarity
Santo santo santo
All the santos, all the santas
Christ
You, Mother Conception
Mother Patroness
Our Mother Mary of Mercy
Our Mother Mary of Mercy
Holy Child of Atocha
You, Moon
You, Cross Star woman, Principal Star woman
You, Moon
You, Morning Star woman, Principal Star woman, Cross Star woman
All the santos
You, my Father
You, Old One
You come here, you come to arrange things, my Father Christ
As you took breath, my Father

As you rested, my Father
So we are going to rest, to take breath
With freshness, with clarity, with light, with the day
Christ
Mother Guadalupe
Mother Conception
Mother Patroness
Mother Nativity
Mother Conception

I am a diviner woman, says
I am a woman who searches, says
Ah, Jesus Christ
I am a lord eagle woman, says
I am an opossum woman, says
I am a woman who sees, says
Ah, Jesus Christ
I am a clean woman, says
She is a woman who resounds, says
She is a woman torn up out of the ground, says
I am an Apostle woman beneath the water, says
I am an Apostle woman beneath the ocean, says
I am a shooting star woman, says
I am a woman like a wolf, says

["You see?" she says to Cayetano. "Yes," he answers. "Isn't that how?" "Yes, it is." Then after a pause she says, "What's so difficult about doing that?"]

Translation from Mazatec into Spanish by Álvaro Estrada and Eloina Estrada de González. English translation by Henry Munn with the assistance of Nati Estrada.

THE 1970 SESSION

THREE EXCERPTS

*This session was given by María Sabina and her niece María Aurora in July 1970
in the house of Celerino Cerqueda and his wife Julia of Huautla de Jiménez, Oaxaca.
The chants were recorded by the host, and no foreigners were present.*

1

I am a saint woman, says
I am a trumpet woman, says
I am a drum woman, says
I am a woman born, says
I am a woman fallen into the world, says
That is your Book, says
That is your Book, says
Book of sap, says
Book of dew, says
Fresh Book, says
Book of clarity, says
Woman of sap, says
Lord of good will, says
Father of the dew, says
Father of the harvest, says

Rich Father, says

Green Father, says

All powerful Father, says

God the Son and Holy Spirit

There is no problem

Her children are crying, her babies are crying, says

I am a woman who looks into the insides of things and investigates, says

I am a woman of sap, says

I am a woman of the dew, says

I am a green woman, says

I am a woman of clarity, says

There is nobody who frightens us, says

There is nobody hovering around, says

I am a woman who cleans, says

That is your Book, says

That is your paper and your Book, says

One and only Father, says

Reasonable Father, says

Father of the dew, says

Fresh Father, says

Father of clarity, says

Holy Father

Beneath the gaze of our Father, says

Beneath the gaze of the person with the staff and the baton of authority,
    says

Yes it's certain, says

It's true, says

I am a woman who looks into the insides of things and investigates, says

The tracks of his hands and his feet, says

The path of sap and dew

The path of freshness and clarity
The path of goodness and the day
I am the one who examines the tracks of the feet and the hands, says
Holy Father, says
It is nothing bad, says
It is with good will, says
It is only in order to enliven and renew life
These are my babies, says
These are my children, says
They are my buds, says
They are my offshoots, says
I am only asking, examining, says
About his business as well
I begin in the depths of the water
I begin where the principal sounds forth, where the sacred sounds forth
I feel very good, says
Healthy
My race is very good, says
What is of value is the ceremony, what is of value is gold, says
Father, says
Santo, says
Santa, says
Santa, says
I am a woman who looks into the insides of things and investigates, says
The tracks of the feet, says
The path of sap and dew, says
In this way it is taught to the children, says
In this way it is taught to our people, says
Where their enjoyment is, their well-being, says
It is health and life, says

We don't want anyone to break our bond and our root, says
Root of sap and of dew, says
Root of greenness and clarity, says

2

I am a little launch woman, says
I am a little shooting star woman, says
I am the Morning Star woman, says
I am the First Star woman, says
I am a woman who goes through the water, says
I am a woman who goes through the ocean, says
I am the great Woman of the Flowing Water, says
I am the sacred Woman of the Flowing Water, says
Where our people are, our powerful people, our important people, says
Our people of reason, says
Holy Father, says
Our Archbishop of Clean Water, says
Our Nun of Clean Water, says
Our Member of the Sisterhood of Clean Water, says
Where you were strewn, Sainted Pope, says
All powerful, one and only Father, says
Father of sap and dew, says

3

I am a shooting star woman, says
I am a trumpet woman, says
I am a drum woman, says
I am a woman violinist, says

Because I am a woman of letters, says
Because I am a Book woman, says
That is your Book, says
Where our Principal Ones are, says
Our people of reason, says
Beer of value, says
Beer, says
My one and only Father, says
Beer that my friends drink, says
Beer that the Archbishop drinks, says
And my Nun also, says
My member of the Sisterhood, says
Archbishop of Clean Water, says
The sainted Pope, says
There I am, says
That is your paper, says
That is your Book, says
Because we are the children of God, says
We are the children of Christ, says
. . . .
I am a woman general, says
I am a woman corporal, says
Holy Father, says
I am a woman corporal, says
I am a lawyer woman, says
A woman of transactions, says
I'm not afraid, says
I'm going to demonstrate my courage, says
Benito Juárez, says
Our Mother Guadalupe, says

Our Mother Magdalene, says
Our Holy Father, says
I am a woman general, says
I am a sergeant woman, says
I am a corporal woman, says
I am a woman commander, says
I am a lawyer woman, says
I am a woman of transactions, says
It comes from the great expanse of the waters, from the expanse
    of the divine sea, says
I go up to heaven, says
Beneath the gaze of your glory, says
There is your paper and your Book, says
That is the best quill, says
That is the best Book, says

Translation from Mazatec into Spanish by
Eloina Estrada de González.
English translation by Henry Munn.

THE MUSHROOM VELADA

THREE EXCERPTS

*Excerpts here are from the curing session performed by María Sabina
on the night of July 12–13, 1958, at the house of Cayetano García, síndico
of Huautla de Jiménez. She was supported on this occasion by her daughter
María Apolonia, herself a curandera, and by Aurelio Carreras, whom
Wasson describes as "a genuine curandero [but] on a much humbler level."*

1

Woman who is more than human am I, he says,[1]
Lawyer woman am I, he says,
Woman of affairs am I, he says, yes, Jesus Christ says,
Yes, Jesus says, I only throw about, I only scatter, he says,
Woman of Puebla am I, he says,
Woman with "balls" am I, he says,
Important eagle woman am I, he says,
Clock woman am I, he says,

---

1. The repeated "he says" here represents the Mazatec particle *-tso,* a grammatical marker indicating direct quotation of another person or being. Elsewhere in these pages Henry Munn translates it simply as "says," since there is no indication here of gender or number. [J.R.]

I am going to show my valor, he says,
I am going to show my valor, he says,
Even before your eyesight, your glory, he says,
Woman who waits am I, he says,
When I shall show my valor, he says,
I am a woman who is more than human, he says,
Yes Jesus Christ says, yes Jesus says,
No one frightens me, he says,
No one is two-faced to me, he says,
Yes Jesus says, yes Jesus says,
Music woman am I, he says,
And drummer woman am I, he says,
Woman violinist am I, he says,
Yes, Jesus Christ says,
Woman of the principal star am I, he says,
Woman of the star of God am I, he says,
Woman of the star of the [Southern] Cross, he says,
Launch [canoe] woman am I, he says, yes Jesus Christ says,
Woman chief of the "clowns" am I, he says, yes Jesus Christ says,
No one frightens me, he says, no one is two-faced to me, he says,
Woman who is more than human am I, he says,
Lawyer woman am I, he says,
And I am going to the sky, he says, yes Jesus Christ says,
Woman [male] saint am I, he says,
I am going to burn the world, he says, yes Jesus Christ says,
I am going to burn the world, he says, yes Jesus Christ says,
Woman of shooting stars am I, he says,
And Saint Peter woman am I, he says,
Whirling woman of the whirlwind am I, he says,
Woman of a sacred, enchanted place am I, he says, yes Jesus Christ says,

Woman [male] saint am I, he says, spirit woman am I, he says,
Illuminated woman am I, he says, yes Jesus says,
I am going to burn the world, he says

2

for Cayetano García

Head of the house, chief of the shade,
Manager of the wind, chief of the thunder,
With calmness, Cayetano García,
Mother Guadalupe, Mother princess,
Woman admired, brilliant woman,
As with calmness, with care,
Whose name is Cayetano García,
You, little Guadalupe,
Woman of the house, woman of the shade,
Woman who walks with the heel, woman of the patio,
Thus you are head of the house, head of the shade,
Chief of the door, chief of the patio,
Cayetano García ... , little Guadalupe ... ,
Father Jesus Christ,
My thoughts are satisfied.
"Little" Cayetano García, "little" Guadalupe ...
As my heart is satisfied,
I am poor, I am humble, Father,
I am poor, I am humble, Christ,
I go with my heel, with my feet,

I go on my knees of sin,
On my knees of tortillas, on my knees of water,
With calmness, with breast milk,
I am going all the way there before stopping, my patron Mother,
I am going to the sky ... Jesus, Jesus, Father ...
There I go always, there I go always,
He who is called Cayetano García, mother Guadalupe,
Look my hands are placed, look my hands are placed,
Look I go on my knees of tortillas, knees of water,
On my knees of sin, Father,
Look I am praying even before your eyes, Father.

3

A Duet, Mother and Daughter

MARÍA SABINA

Christ! ... before your eyes, before your mouth,
We speak with humility, with beseechings to Christ.

MARÍA APOLONIA

Oh Mary, oh most holy Mary,
We will only thunder, he says, we will only sound, he says,
We will only shout, he says, we will only whistle, he says.

MARÍA SABINA

Saint Peter, Saint Paul.

MARÍA APOLONIA

For there is the medicine flower, he says,
The medicinal leaves, he says.

MARÍA SABINA

The flower of breast milk, the dew flower.

MARÍA APOLONIA

Go with thirteen hummingbirds, he says, lord of the birds,
    he says, lord of the holy birds, he says.

MARÍA SABINA

Fresh flower, tender flower,

MARÍA APOLONIA

I am going ...

MARÍA SABINA

Go with breast milk, with dew,

MARÍA APOLONIA

Even unto the sky, he says, unto glory, he says.

MARÍA SABINA

María Apolonia!

MARÍA APOLONIA

You Father whose the sky is,
You papa whose the world is, oh Mary,
Woman who sounds forth,
Powerful woman who sounds forth.

Translation by George M.
and Florence H. Cowan

COMMENTARIES & DERIVATIONS

INTRODUCTION TO *THE LIFE*
OF MARÍA SABINA

ÁLVARO ESTRADA

It was not only the gold and natural riches of Anáhuac, the culture and art of Mesoamerica that astonished the Spanish priests and conquistadores who arrived in this land in the sixteenth century: the native medicines (comprising a "marvelous collection" of hallucinogenic plants) were also the objects of attention, study, and condemnation on the part of European writers, botanists, and doctors during the colonial epoch in Mexico.

First the repressions exercised by the Tribunal of the Holy Office against those who resorted to the ingestion of *ololiuhqui, peyotl,* or *teonanácatl* ("seeds, cactus, or mushrooms," all of them hallucinogenic), and then centuries of condemnations from the pulpit forced native doctors to shift the rites and worship of the magical plants onto a private, even secret, plane.

In our day, those "demoniacal" practices of the Indians have been disappearing with the advance of Western culture in Mexico. The same phenomenon has extinguished similar customs among other Asiatic and American peoples. Yet in Huautla—a town situated in the Sierra Mazatec of the Mexican state of Oaxaca—investigators have found a mine for the study of this type of native practice. There the mushroom—to which the investigators have added the adjective "hallucinogenic"—is central to the indigenous religion in which it is said that the ancient *teonanácatl*—"Flesh of the Gods" in the pre-Hispanic epoch—not only has the power to cure all sicknesses but gives the mystical force that creates the elevated, esoteric language of the shaman.

During trance, the *Wise One* (the name the Mazatecs give to the shaman) speaks, invoking tribal as well as Christian deities (testimony to the inescapable syncretism of our time).

Did anyone write about the hallucinogenic plants and their use before their recent rediscovery? The ethnomycologist R. Gordon Wasson writes: "The references that we find in Mexico to the specific use of *teonanácatl* by the Mexican Indians are valuable but incomplete. Sahagún, Motolinía, Diego Durán, Father de la Serna, the learned Ruiz de Alarcón, Tezozomoc, and Don Francisco Hernández, the botanist and doctor of Philip II, all wrote about the subject. Without doubt the informants of the chroniclers didn't tell all they knew about the various hallucinogenic plants they were aware of and used, because they were impeded by the principle of not revealing religious secrets to anyone from outside the community. Now it is known that the ingestion of such plants was always connected with religion. Every religion has secrets; even the Christian religion speaks of *mysteries*" (personal communication).

In his book *Medicine and Magic,* Dr. Gonzalo Aguirre Beltrán writes: "The distorted vision displayed by such famous writers as Hernando Ruiz de Alarcón, Jacinto de la Serna, and Pedro Ponce, when they touch this fundamental aspect of native medicine, is easy to explain in individuals whose religious principles prevent them from seeing anything but the work of the devil—the helpless and maligned devil—in Indian mysticism."

In brief, we find that the natives neither revealed all that they knew nor were the chroniclers able to divest themselves of their prejudices sufficiently to leave an impartial, objective testimony to the cult with which the ancient Mexicans surrounded the Flesh of the Gods.

The motives that prompted my decision to write *The Life of María Sabina* were: (1) the intention of leaving a testimony to the thought and life of the Mazatec *Wise Woman* whom journalists and writers from various countries have not known how to appreciate fully; (2) the hope that it may be a useful document for ethnologists, ethnomycologists, students of folklore, and other specialists; and (3) to give the general public a better idea of the native customs, and encourage young people in particular to treat the elements of the native religion with more respect. It is my hope, too, that this work may stimulate young writers—above all, Indians—to study such native customs in order to rescue them from their approaching definitive extinction.

The present manuscript is the result of a series of interviews that I conducted sporadically from September 1975 to August 1976. During this time my professional duties as an engineer, which made it necessary for me to live in Mexico City, alternated with visits to Huautla to converse with María Sabina. Mine has not been an easy task even though I am a native of Huautla and speak Mazatec.

To make it easier for the reader, I have omitted the questions that I asked María Sabina, although I have kept the tapes on which the Mazatec Wise Woman's words were recorded.

In the final writing of the text, as throughout this project, I have been conscious of the responsibility incurred in writing down the autobiography of a person who, because she can neither read nor write and does not even speak Spanish, could never herself know with exactitude whether what has been written about her is correct or not.

Mexico, D.F., September 4, 1976

I met María Sabina in Huautla in 1967 at the house of a sister of mine. She was seated on the floor, leaning against the inside partition of boards of a typical Mazatec hut that served as a kitchen. I'm not exaggerating if I say that when I greeted her I felt her look charged with mystery and light. Afterwards I grew accustomed to perceiving this strange look.

On one occasion in 1970 when I visited her, she showed me an official paper from the town hall notifying her that she was being summoned for a judicial investigation because, according to what she told me, a local troublemaker had accused her of selling marijuana, a story he had made up to distract the authorities since in reality it was he who was involved in that business. I brought her to Mexico City where

I was studying engineering. I hid her with some relatives for more than a month. Finally, I decided to take her to a reporter for the then-influential magazine *¡Siempre!* The interview attracted the attention of the government of the state of Oaxaca, and she was exonerated of all guilt.

The magazine reporter was impressed by the way in which I talked directly to María Sabina in our native language, for which reason he suggested to me that I write her biography. At that time I was contributing articles and reports to the same magazine, *¡Siempre!* The idea of writing the life of the señora appeared to me a difficult task, especially since the writer Fernando Benítez had already published a brief biography, in which he identified her as a shaman, and Gordon Wasson had also published his *Mazatec Mushroom Velada*. Nevertheless, I decided to write the biography of the señora, seeing that she had not been completely understood by those who made her known to the world. Even some names of her relatives weren't exact. I had to go to the town church to obtain her baptism certificate.

I began my interviews with María Sabina by means of a questionnaire that I went on enriching and amplifying in the course of eleven months (September 1975 to August 1976). As I moved ahead on the manuscript I arranged the biography chronologically. I turned to other people, old people mostly, in order for them to explain to me more fully what the shaman of Huautla had told me. That happened in those cases in which I had doubts or which referred to certain ancestral customs—that of the agricultural ceremony, for example.

On finishing the text I polished it various times before sending it to Gordon Wasson, whom I had met in Mexico City in 1975 and to whom I had promised to send it. (Our initial meeting was in the house of Henry Munn.) Wasson then asked the Mexican poet Octavio Paz for his opinion of the manuscript. Paz expressed his appreciation for the work: he said it was a document with anthropological and human value. Notwithstanding, he suggested that the author eliminate terms and words that didn't seem in accord with the personality of María Sabina, both in the text and in the translation of the chants. He suggested greater simplicity in the words, and in a letter to Wasson, he said that one ought to give the literal meaning of the shaman's words without it mattering whether the reader understood them or not.

It was the editor of the subsequent book who asked me to translate the chants on the Folkways record, recorded by Mr. Wasson in 1956. That was another surprise for me, that the first North American translators—Protestant missionaries settled in Huautla who had learned to speak the Mazatec language—had not completely understood the words of María Sabina. The translation by the missionaries came in the liner notes inserted in the record jacket. I found that for the most part the actual chants of María Sabina were far removed from the version of the missionaries, Eunice V. Pike and Sarah Gudshinsky.

Once the text was finished and corrected in line with Octavio Paz's suggestions, I gave the definitive manuscript to the Siglo XXI publishing company. The essay on María Sabina by her discoverer Gordon Wasson was also a valuable contribution.

I never thought that the biography of María Sabina would have the success it has had in being translated into various languages around the world.

June 2001
Translation from Spanish
by Henry Munn

from T E O - N A N Á C A T L :

T H E   M U S H R O O M   *A G A P E*

VALENTINA PAVLOVNA WASSON

AND R. GORDON WASSON

[1957] María Sabina is a woman in her fifties, grave in demeanor, with a grave smile, short of stature like all Mazatecs, dressed in the Mazatec *huipil.* Her daughter is in her thirties and in all respects takes after her mother. She is following her mother's vocation. The Señora herself is at the peak of her powers, and it is easy to see why Guadalupe had said to us of her that she was *una Señora sin mancha,* a lady without blemish, immaculate, one who had never dishonored her calling by using her powers for evil. She alone, said Guadalupe, had brought the latter's children through all the diseases that take a frightful toll in early childhood in the Mazatec country. After that initial talk we were to pass two all-night vigils with Doña María and her daughter, and we can testify that she is a woman of rare moral and spiritual power, dedicated in her vocation, an artist in her mastery of the techniques of her office. It was her example that drove home for us for the first time a rule that must govern all field anthropologists. In the archaic cultures as among advanced peoples, there is a hierarchy of excellence when it comes to the individuals who are the culture-bearers. It is not sufficient to rely on the first informants that present themselves, on any shaman who is willing to talk. The whole cultural area must be dis-

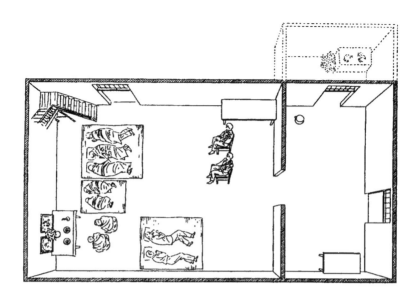

creetly surveyed and communication must be established with the finest exponents of the old traditions. None of the formidable difficulties of physical existence in these remote regions nor of communication should be permitted to blunt this obligation.

[...]

There were a few home-made wooden chairs in the room, and in the beginning Allan [Richardson] and RGW used them. Cayetano's brother Genaro and possibly one other remained seated on chairs the whole night through. The others lay or reclined on mats on the floor, wrapped in *sarapes,* except of course for the Señora and her daughter, who, wearing clean *huipiles* with identical reddish-yellow birds embroidered on them in front, sat before the altar-table on mats. They sat with what seemed a half-studied formality, the daughter a little behind her mother and slightly to her mother's right. Later, in the dark, we could barely discern their triangular shadows as first one and then the other lifted her voice in song.

[...]

After the Señora had put out the last *vela,* a silence of perhaps twenty minutes followed. The moon was shining brightly outside, and its orbit was such that the shaft of moonlight entering above the door fell squarely on the altar-table, but it did little to relieve the general darkness in the room. Suddenly the Señora began to moan, low at first, then louder. There were silent pauses, and then renewed humming. Then the humming stopped and she began to articulate isolated syllables, each syllable consisting of a consonant followed by a vowel, sharply pronounced. The syllables came snapping out in rapid succession, cutting the darkness like a knife, spoken, not shouted. After a time the syllables coalesced into what we took for words, and the Señora began to chant. The chanting continued intermittently all night, first by the Señora and then by her daughter, and afterwards alternately by one or the other. The chanting was in Mazatec, and there was no one to translate the words for us. Neither Allan nor RGW is instructed musicologically, and we cannot say whether the provenience of the music was European or indigenous. That the chanting was in Mazatec, and not in Latin or Spanish learned by rote, adds point to this question. (If the chants are old, the language may be archaic, which would be a discovery of high interest for the handful of first-rate scholars who have devoted themselves to Mazatec linguistics.) Both women chanted in that distinctive way which seems always to mark the intoning of age-old chants; the singing was soaked in weary melancholy. Our Señora's voice was not loud, probably not loud enough to be heard in the village thoroughfare. But there was a confidence and resonance in her utterance that imposed itself. There came a moment late in the night when the Señora made her way to the door on the terrace and went outside, holding her hand on the door. (To this extent she was free of the prohibition laid on the rest of us not to leave the house.) When she re-entered, she left the door slightly ajar, and we saw her advance *on her knees* across the open space in the room, and then turn to the right toward the altar-table. Her hands were uplifted to shoulder-level, palms exposed. As she slowly progressed, she sang a canticle that seemed like an introit, indescribably tender and plaintive in its musical phrases. Her daughter sang well too, but lacked her authority. From time to time, as they sang, the men who had taken the mushrooms, notably Genaro and young Emilio, ejaculated words, groans, short sentences, and vocal noises. We know not what they said, but they seemed to intervene with their voices to suit the singing, in such a way as to produce a strange, barbaric harmony.

The singing was not continuous. For stretches the Señora would talk, as though invoking the Spirits or as though the Holy Ghost was speaking through the mushrooms. We heard the names of Christ (which she pronounced with an intrusive "r," *Khristros*), of St. Peter and St. Paul. We heard her cry out "Pedro" repeatedly in an imploring tone, and knew that the mushrooms were wrestling with the problem of Peter. Emilio made his way to us and whispered that Peter was alive and well, and contrite for not having let us hear from him. We asked for further details, but Emilio said that since we ourselves had eaten the mushrooms, we could expect them to speak to us directly. Our interpreter Emilio then vanished into the darkness for the rest of the night.

Unlike the chants, the spoken utterances were fresh and vibrant and rich in expressiveness. The mushrooms were talking to the point. We had never suspected how sensitive and poetic an instrument the Mazatec language could be. The intermittent snatches of the Señora's monologue seemed quick with subtle feeling, laden with dramatic import. In our very presence a priestess of the old religion was pronouncing oracular dictates in spurts, hot and firm with authority.

How we regretted that we had no means to record her voice! (At the time we asked ourselves, and we have repeated the question often since then, whether our critical faculties were deranged by the effects of the mushrooms, so that we over-rated the quality of the Señora's performance. Perhaps so. But if this is an aberration, typical of the syndrome of mushroomic ecstasy, our account at least serves to document it for the record, and to establish that our hallucinations were auditory as well as visual.)

The chanting and the oracular utterances turned out to be only a part of what we were to witness. At an early stage we sensed that the Señora was either kneeling or standing before the altar-table gesticulating with her arms. We detected this by ear and confirmed it uncertainly with the aid of the meager moonlight. Then, much later in the night when her daughter took over the chanting, the Señora made her way to the open space between us and the door, and she embarked on a kind of dance that must have lasted for two hours or more. We do not know precisely what she did, because of the darkness, but she was between us and the aperture above the door, and we could just make out that she was turning clock-wise, facing in succession each of the four compass points, at the same time raising and lowering her arms. Her daughter was singing, but she was not silent. She was engaged in a lengthy, rhythmic percussive utterance of a kind unfamiliar to us. There was a differentiation in the pitch of the beats, and at times the pattern or phrases seemed to us complex. We cannot say for sure how she made her sounds, but we are almost sure that she clapped her hands, slapped her knees, smacked her forehead, and whammed her chest. We were impressed by the cleanness of the utterance. Every clap or slap or smack or wham was resonant. Remembering the role played by pitch in the Mazatec language, we asked ourselves whether the Señora was speaking percussively. On each of our two nights with her, she rinsed her mouth once with water, and the gargling was also rhythmic, and perhaps tonally differentiated. Then she would spit out the water on the ground unrhythmically. On Saturday night, in a moment of illumination by flashlight, we saw and heard her twicking her long fingernails rhythmically. A remarkable feature of her percussive utterance on Wednesday night was its ventriloquistic property. For a long stretch we were in the blackest darkness while the daughter sang and the Señora was performing her strange dance with percussive accompaniment. As she would snap out her resonant claps and smacks, we seemed to catch them out of the night from various directions. Let the reader remember that all the while we were seeing our visions *and* attending to the auditory sensations served to us by the two women. There we were, visually suspended in space before the vast panorama of, say, the Gobi Desert, with a singing accompaniment and with percussive cracks assailing us, now from above, now here, now there, exactly like Hamlet's ghost *hic et ubique,* hitting us with a cutting crispness from unpredictable quarters, as though an air-borne choir of invisible creatures was peopling the dark void around us, perplexing us with their assorted and shifting cries. Possibly this ventriloquistic effect was caused by the Señora's turning in different directions as she performed, so that the sound caromed to us from the ceiling or walls. And all the while there was the irregular chorus, subdued in volume, of ecstatic exclamations from the Indians reclining on the ground. Confined though we were in a room without windows or open door, at one point we felt a swish of air, just as though we were really suspended in the great outdoors. Was this too an hallucination? If so, all shared it, for when the wind blew on us, there was general excitement, flashlights were switched on, and our Indian friends were sitting up, amazed at being stroked by the Divine Afflatus.

[...]

At intervals throughout the night, perhaps every forty minutes or so, there would be what we can only describe as intermissions. After working up to a powerful climax in utterance, the Señora and her daughter would subside into silence. We recall one such climax when the Señora, half-singing, half-declaiming, spat forth in endless repetition and with barbaric violence the two syllables chung-ha (the first element rhyming, not with [English] "sung" but with the Chinese "Sung"); we were never able to learn what this meant. After such climaxes our two votaries and our reclining Indian friends would light cigarettes (ordinary ones) and smoke and engage in the most animated conversation. Clearly they were discussing what was happening, but we had no interpreter. They would light the electric torches. We took advantage of these moments to study the Señora. She was not in a trance. That is to say, she was one of us, talking and smoking. But she was in a state of excitement, her eyes flashing, her smile no longer that grave smile which we had observed before, but now quick with animation and, if we may use the word, *caritas*. For there is another aspect to the mushrooms that we must mention. The spirit of an *agape* of which we have already spoken was a prelude to a wave of generous or tender feelings that the mushrooms aroused in everyone. To illustrate this, we recall how, when nausea first sent one of us into the adjoining room to vomit, the Señora, who had been in full song, immediately stopped the performance, and she and the others manifested the most embarrassing solicitude about the unhappy episode, which after all was wholly unimportant. On the two nights that we passed in Cayetano's house, we were aware of no erotic stimulation among those present and we think there was none. But the feeling of brotherly affection was strong indeed. Twice in the course of that first night the Señora reached out her right hand to RGW and sought contact with his fingers in friendly greeting, across the chasm of the language barrier.

THE UNIQUENESS
OF MARÍA SABINA

HENRY MUNN

*An independent scholar and writer, Henry Munn arrived in Huautla for the
first time in 1965. His essays on Mazatec religion and related subjects have
appeared in anthologies published by Oxford University Press and the University
of California Press and in journals such as* Plural *(edited by Octavio Paz),*
The CoEvolution Quarterly, New Wilderness Letter, *and the* Journal of
Latin American Lore. *He is presently completing a book on Mazatec shamanic
chants, and other works-in-progress include a reading of some scenes in the
pre-Columbian Mixtec codices and an extensive autobiographical narrative.*

Since María Sabina is the most renowned Mazatec shaman, people
tend to think she is the only one, not realizing that she is part of a liv-
ing tradition. A comparison of her chants with those of four other
shamans I recorded in Huautla between 1967 and 1980 (one woman
and three men) shows the similarities between her vocabulary and
theirs and at the same time throws into relief what makes her differ-
ent from them.

The form of the chant—short enunciations ending with *tso,* "it
says," like a vocal punctuation mark in the flow of speech, a reference
to the voice speaking through them—is used by all Mazatec shamans,

especially when they shift from speech into song. It is a cultural creation: a way of canalizing the energy released.

Shamans also share a vocabulary and a stock of standardized expressions that they draw on in their chants. "Slowly and with care / with sap, with dew / with greenness, with clarity," María Sabina says again and again over the sick boy during the Wasson velada. *Ho nca inta, ho nca nangui*—"slowly and with care," literally with one's feet on the ground—is said to people when they set out on a journey. It is one of the expressions commonly used as well by the shamans. The cluster of words—*ntsin,* "sap," the milk inside a plant; *xoñon,* "dew"; *xcoen,* "green" in the sense of fresh and tender (the color green is *sase*); and *yova,*[1] "clarity"—expresses the quintessence of the Mazatec shamans' illuminated sense of nature. They all use these words in different combinations in their chants.

Two other words that go together in the chants of María Sabina and those of the other Mazatec curanderos are *yo*—the buds of a flower; and *chi꜔nte*—tender in the sense of what is young, newborn, a plant just shooting up. Mrs. Eloina Estrada de González, who translated the recordings for me, translated this couplet as "offshoots and tenderness." In the chants of María Sabina I render them as "buds and sprouts." These words, which refer to the stages of growth of plants, are used as metaphors for babies and children. This is the view of life of an agricultural community.

"Grace, goodness" (*khoa nta*) and "life and well-being" (*khoa vihna, khoa visen*) are correlated in the parallel constructions of the shamanic chants with "sap and dew," "greenness and clarity." The opposites of these four kernel words are "garbage and dust" (*tje, chao*), "whirlwind

1. Transliteration from Mazatec. For a note on Mazatec orthography, see page 47, note 11. [J.R.]

and wind" (*xquin, ntjao*)—figures of speech for sickness and disputes. María Sabina frequently asserts that the work of her "saints," meaning the mushrooms, is to dispel them and clear the air.

Her words go together in couplets. These double expressions in which the same thing is said twice in different ways are a characteristic of pre-Hispanic Mesoamerican rhetoric. Other common stereotyped expressions that recur from shaman to shaman follow this same pattern: *ngui xcoin, ngui ntso?vai*—"beneath your eyes, beneath your mouth"; *ma* and *tao*—"poor and humble (or loved)"; *tsin ḵhoa?aon, tsin ḵhoa?nte*—"there is no resentment, there is no rancor"; *cjain ni, ḵishiḵhoa ni*—"it is certain, it is true."

They all inherit from their culture a repertory of themes and motifs on which each one works his or her own individual variations. When María Sabina says she is a *chjon chjine xḵi, chjon chjine xca, chjon chjine en, chjon chjine ḵhoa*—"a woman wise in medicine, a woman wise in herbs, a woman wise in words, a woman wise in problems"— she is stating her culture's concept of the shaman's role. The other Mazatec *chota chjine*—"wise ones"—all define themselves in exactly the same terms.

She often says, "I am a woman of the light, I am a woman of the day." Here she is playing on the Mazatec word for spirit, *sennichi,* by breaking it down into its two component parts: *sen*—physiognomy or light, depending on how it is used; and *nich i*—day, the destiny of a person determined by the day sign of his or her birth (the Mazatec equivalent of the Aztec *tonalli,* which meant light, heat, day, and spirit). She usually says before or afterwards, "I am a woman *espíritu,*" translating the native concept into Spanish. Other shamans do the same thing. Another wise woman prays, "Bring his appearance, bring his day." A shaman from Loma de Chapultepec on the slopes of the sacred mountain opposite Huautla speaks of "the path of the cane of office, the path of the staff, the path of the light, the path of the day (*ntia ya, ntia nise, ntia sen, ntia nichi*) of each of his patients.

She herself says of her host during the Folkways session that he is a "man with a green staff, a staff of clarity (*nise xcoen, nise yova*)." The words of a medicine man from Xochitonalco, a hamlet near Huautla, recall hers; he says to the old couple he is speaking for, "You should take your staff of dew, your staff of fragrant leaves. Grace, life, and well-being. Green staff, staff of clarity (*nise xcoen, nise yova*)." The leaves he is referring to are those used in the steam bath to hit the body so as to make the air circulate.

The path is a common motif in the chants of the Mazatec shamans who live in a mountain world of footpaths where people leave the tracks of their bare feet in the brown, squishy mud. The experience takes the form of a "trip." One function of the shamanic chant is to guide the effect of the mushrooms on the participants and lead them by suggestion along a good path to a healing, cathartic experience. María Sabina speaks frequently of following in the footsteps of Christ. Compare her words with those of the medicine man from Xochitonalco: "It is life and well-being of our Father, says. It is sap and dew, says. It is buds and tenderness, says. It is the path of the tracks, it is the path of the feet of our Christ, says." Sometimes the path is that of the extravagated spirit of the sick, which has to be followed to where the person was frightened. The Wise Woman sings, "We are going looking for the path, the path of his paws, the path of his claws, from the right side to the left side we are going to work, says." The shaman from the Loma de Chapultepec, sitting in a chair before the family altar in the house where he has been called to give a ceremony, states, "The work I came for is to divine for them, how they are in their door, their dooryard, the path of the tracks of their feet." At one moment in the Folkways session, María Sabina says: "I am going to receive there in the path / I am going to receive the enchantment / I am going to receive his light, his day / the path of his soles, the path of his feet." She means she is going to reintegrate the person with his or her *sennichi-li*. For her the path of the hands and the feet is what one does, where one goes.

In Huautla people would explain the similarities in vocabulary and figures of speech between different shamans by saying that it is the mushrooms speaking through them. I don't think we can accept that explanation, which from the scientific point of view is a personification into an imaginary entity of the unconscious powers of language. None of the curanderos and curanderas I recorded had heard each other speak, but they had all at one time or another in the past heard other shamans give ceremonies, either when they were children or when they were sick and had to be cured. The uncanny way the couplets of the shamanic chant imprint themselves on the memory of ordinary listeners, even when the exact meaning of the words is beyond them, suggests how the liturgy of the mushroom medicine rites has been transmitted from generation to generation.

When María Sabina was a child, she heard shamans sing, like many Mazatec children who have lain awake at night listening to the strange words of medicine men and women singing in the darkness under the din of the rain on the thatch roof or with the chirp of the crickets in the background. The raw psycho-physiological experience is shaped by cultural models. When she began to eat the mushrooms, she already knew the form of the chant and the type of things that are said.

What then distinguishes her from her contemporaries?

First of all, her musicality. Within the traditional framework of the ritual, developed to utilize the psychoactive medicine for therapeutic social purposes, each shaman has his or her own magic song, distinctive voice, personal melody, and individual manner of conducting a ceremony. Nevertheless, the melodiousness of María Sabina's chants, their rhythmical transporting effect, is unsurpassed except at moments by other singers.

The effect of the mushrooms she has eaten for the power to cure makes the body vibrate. Hence her humming—a way of tuning herself in to the energy flowing through her. When she invokes the Virgins and the Saints, she draws out the endings of their names into reverberant tones. At the same time she marks the intensified pulse beat of her physical existence by clapping and uttering sequences of vocables: ecstatic phonation, articulatory play, a vocalization of impulses, a rhythmical syllabification of energy.

So so so si are the component parts of *Jesusi,* a common exclamation of Mazatec women. *Ki ko ka ka ki* form *Kristo. Ma ma ma mai* become *madre.* The syllables are used as beats; meaning is broken down into pure sounds and recomposed from them. The vocables sometimes seem to go back to the babble of babies. In her repetition of *santo santa* the binary alternation of sounds is what she likes, the contrast of *to* and *ta.* This is a level of vocalization I have heard in no other Mazatec shaman. The large part played by percussion, humming, and the enunciation of syllables in her ceremonies exemplifies her expressionistic creativity and distinguishes her performances from those of her contemporaries.

What is not on the printed page is the sensorial condition of heightened sensitivity in which her words are spoken and heard: their resonance. In many passages the lilt of her voice carries a force, conveys a sense of enthusiasm that is not present in just the words themselves. It is the music of the shamanic chant, its rhythm and melody, that moves the listeners as much as the words and cures them by the power of song to uplift and transport the soul.

María Sabina alone of all the shamans says, "I am a trumpet

woman, I am a drum woman, I am a woman violinist." Her words
bring to mind the mushroom ceremony pictured at the center of the
Codex Vindobonensis obverse, an ancient Mixtec pictographic book
from an area of what is now the state of Oaxaca not far from the Maza-
tec mountains. In it, 9 Wind—the Mixtec culture hero who is dressed
in the attributes of the wind deity the Aztecs called Quetzalcoatl—is
shown officiating as a shaman, playing on a rasp with a human skull
for a resonator, the volutes of speech coming out of his mouth.

Wasson describes her dancing as she sings, turning around in the
middle of the dark room, lifting her arms in gestures of adoration and
imploration. Her activity of expression is total: musical and gestural
as well as verbal. The whole body speaks. Listening to her talk in or-
dinary life, without understanding what she was saying, I was struck
by the idiosyncratic gestures she would make with her hands and
fingers. Of all living Mazatec shamans, María Sabina was unques-
tionably the greatest because of her radical, extreme personality.

One of the most distinctive features of her chants is how she as-
sumes the being of the phenomena she names by saying "I am" this or
that. One shaman—by day a shopkeeper in the market—asserted, "I
am he who speaks with the mountains" (a male prerogative; the
women kneel on their mats, imploring), but even though he evoked
eagles and vortices of colors, he did not identify with them. The level
of discourse of the other *chota chjine* is practical, functional. They
emphasize what they do—cure—and what they want—to get rid of
sickness. In none of the chants of the other shamans I have recorded
does the "I am" have the same importance it does in the words of
María Sabina.

Her identifications are like the masks the Tlingit and Eskimo
shamans put on and took off: bear spirit, deer spirit, moon, kingfisher,
raven, eagle, old woman, cloud spirit, the spirit of the driftwood, even

bubbles. This is Coleridge's "Infinite I am" of the "primary imagination," the "I is an other" of Rimbaud.

She stands out from her contemporaries because of her repertory's wide range of images. They have associations for the Mazatec listener that they don't have for the foreign reader. Let us consider the cultural concepts behind some of them.

EAGLE WOMAN

Frederick Starr, an American physical anthropologist who visited Huautla in 1900, in describing the long dresses of the women, said, "Their huipils are among the most striking we have seen, being made of native cotton, decorated with elaborate embroidered patterns of large size in pink or red. The favorite design is the eagle." From the pictures I have seen of these old dresses, the eagle on the breast was often in the form of the eagle sitting on a prickly pear cactus with a snake in its mouth: the symbol of Mexico. One explanation for María Sabina's constant association of the eagle and the clock in the Wasson velada may be the Mexican national emblem on the Huautla schoolhouse clocktower in front of the church. Like dream images, her ideas have multiple determinants. People on the mushrooms often feel themselves flying through the air, looking down at the earth from high above. The medicine man from Xochitonalco told me, "The eagle is the Mother who is in Heaven." In his chants he spoke of "the jaguar with spots of our Lord Jesus Christ / the big eagle of our Virgin."

CLOCK WOMAN

María Sabina incorporates the modern world into her chants: she is a *chjon reloj*—a clock woman. The association between the eagle and the clock is constant throughout the 1958 session. In the 1970 session, the association shifts to one between the clock and the book, the clock and God. Once when a man from Huautla (an accountant in Mexico City) ate the mushrooms with her, she said, "Son, you have watches all over your body." He said, "No, I have only one." "What she means," explained his mother, "is that you have plenty of time, you have lots of luck."

OPOSSUM WOMAN

The opposite of the eagle, whirling high in the sky, is the opossum who goes along close to the ground: a nocturnal marsupial, a denizen of the cornfield and woodpile. The opossum plays an important role in Mazatec mythology. It stole fire from an old lady who had monopolized it by sticking its tail into the flames and running off with it ablaze like a torch to distribute fire to the first people—which is why the furry animal has a hairless tail. The opossum also plays dead, then jumps up and runs away when nobody is looking. The Huautecans believe it is impossible to kill one except by burning it. Men sometimes eat the heart of an opossum to become invulnerable. When María Sabina calls herself an opossum woman, she almost always says next, *Chjon nka cohon nia*—"I am a woman who sees."

HUMMINGBIRD WOMAN

Hummingbirds, hovering in front of flowers with vibrating wings, are a common sight around Mazatec homes, where there are often tobacco plants—San Pedro—whose pink trumpet-like flowers are visited by the tiny birds with their long bills. María Sabina is the only *chota chjine* whom I have heard invoke hummingbirds. The Mazatec name for them, *tontsin,* emphasizes their vibratory nature, like our word for them in English, unlike the Spanish *chuparrosa,* "rose-sucker." Whenever she mentions them, she calls them *ntsica nai, ntsica chikon*—"lord *ntsica,* sacred *ntsica*"—possibly an onomatopoeic nickname based on their calls or the word for them in a neighboring dialect. We translate it as "colibrí" [hummingbird], while Estrada translates it as "sucker," although the word itself has no relation to the verb "to suck," to give the idea that the birds with their long bills suck nectar from the flowers as the shaman sucks illness out of the patient. His mother once told me that soon after her rheumatism began she ate the mushrooms with María Sabina in hopes of alleviation. At one moment during the night, she saw the curandera far away from her in the darkness, turning around, her huipil billowing out around her, with a long, hollow tube of bamboo in her mouth through which she was sucking the illness out of her. At another moment, she felt that María Sabina was pulling the pains out of her neck and body as she sang, like a rope she coiled up around her shoulder in time to the measures of her song. The next morning Estrada's mother had tobacco between her teeth that the medicine woman had given her to swallow in order to make her vomit.

The hummingbirds are among María Sabina's auxiliary spirits. She calls them "children." This simile has a long history in the Meso-american imagination. Bernardino de Sahagún says in his *Historia general de las cosas de Nueva España* that children who died as babies went to the land of abundance, "where there are all kinds of trees and flowers and fruits and they go about there like *tzintzones* that are little birds of diverse colors that go about sucking the flowers of the trees" (Book 6, Chapter XXI).

The words I've translated as "whirling woman of colors"—*chjon ts?o tji*—literally mean "round (*tji*) huipil (*ts?o*) woman (*chjon*)," but the term has an esoteric meaning familiar to many Huautecans. Several men have described to me how, in the early morning, one sometimes sees along the paths in the mist a whirlwind of colors like a huipil ornamented with ribbons of different colors spinning around. They call this atmospherical phenomenon the *chjon ts?o tji*. When I asked the medicine man from Xochitonalco about it, he said, *ts?o tji nai, ts?o tji chikon,* using the same qualitatives that María Sabina had: principal or lord and sacred. "It's like a rainbow—green, red, white—and it goes along in front of one like a ferris wheel spinning around. When that *cabrón* gets on top of one, the person falls down in an attack. It appears when the clouds are down to the ground." He was as familiar with this optical phenomenon as María Sabina was, but for him it was a malevolent spirit that could cause epileptic attacks—he would never have introduced it into his chants. She had the audacity to identify herself with beings other shamans might be afraid to even name.

SHOOTING STAR WOMAN

Sometimes in the clear mountain nights or just before dawn, looking up at the bright stars, one sees a streak of light that disappears almost as soon as it appears, leaving one with the impression of being lucky enough to have seen a rare cosmic event—a meteor. The shooting star, *chihon-li,* also has esoteric associations. Some people are believed to have this "virtue." They change into shooting stars, dive into mountains, and come back with treasures, but they are usually sickly. Shooting stars are connected with the idea of luck and wealth. At one moment in the 1970 session, sung when she was seventy-six, María Sabina seems to imagine herself traversing the ocean in her *lancha,* "launch," like a shooting star crossing the starry sky.

THE OCEAN

The Mazatecs call the ocean *nta chikon*—"the sacred waters"—like the Aztecs, who called it *teo atl*—"divine water." Sahagún explains that this means "water marvellous in depth and in grandeur," and he says they also called it *ihuicaatl*—"water that joins the sky" (Book 11, Chapter XIII). For the Mazatecs, as for their pre-Hispanic ancestors, heaven is on the other side of the water. A man in the lowland Mazatec region told Carlos Incháustegui, "On the other side of the Ocean is seated God, the eternal Father." This explains many of the passages in María Sabina's chants where she imagines herself going through the water up to heaven.

The American linguist Eunice V. Pike told R. Gordon Wasson, in a 1953 letter from Huautla, speaking about the beliefs of the people with respect to the mushrooms, "Most of them agree that the wise men frequently see the ocean and for these mountain people that is exciting." Álvaro Estrada understood from María Sabina that she sometimes saw herself actually swimming through the water, which she expressed in Mazatec as *nta tson:* "paddle in the water." For her, the idea of being under the water seems to have been a metaphor for the trance from which she spoke her words. In 1970 she says, "I am a woman wise in words beneath the water, I am a woman wise in words beneath the ocean."

During the 1970 session, María Sabina invokes the *Chjon Nta Ve*—the "Woman of the Flowing Water"—who is the principal female deity of Mazatec myth. Depending on the version of the story, she was either the wife or the daughter-in-law of Chikon Tokosho, the lord of the magnificent symmetrical mountain that stands in front of Huautla like a benevolent presence dwelling above the town. One day she is sent to the cornfield to pick corn and comes back with a full sack. Her mother-in-law scolds her for having picked so much. Offended, she leaves the house. But when they go to the milpa they find she had picked only one ear in each corner of the field. "She had cut only one or two ears, but for her they yielded a whole sack full. Probably because she was the *chjon cha?a ntsai, chjon cha?a ntsja,*" said the shaman from Loma de Chapultepec on the slopes of the sacred mountain, who told me her story. He used exactly the same words María Sabina describes her with when she says in 1970, "She is the Woman of the Flowing Water / She is a woman whose palms are like spoons / She is a woman with hands of measure."

It is customary in Huautla for a newly married woman to go to live with her husband's family. The moral of the story is, be careful with daughters-in-law. They may get angry and leave the house, and then you'll miss them. What happens to the *Chjon Nta Ve* on her peregrinations about the mountains gives places their names. Finally she reaches the Río Santo Domingo, which flows through the mountains in a deep canyon that separates the Mazatec watershed from the land of the Cuicatec-speaking people on the other side of the river. There she settles down at a place called *Nta Ve,* a ford where the water runs shallow over the stones. Sometimes her husband, the Lord of the Mountain, goes to visit her. When he does the corn is abundant. One knows he is there because one hears the coyotes—his dogs—howling at night.

María Sabina calls her *chjon cha?a ntsai, chjon cha?a ntsja:* literally, "woman with palms like spoons, woman with hands like spoons." All the Mazatec *chota chjine* refer to her with these same epithets. They mean a woman who knows exactly the right amount of ingredients to put into her cooking. No matter how many guests her husband brings home to eat, she always has enough to go around. This expression is not an invention of María Sabina; it is a cultural concept.

Her clapping during her shamanic sessions is an extension into another modality of the everyday action of Huautla women patting cornmeal between their hands to make tortillas that they lay on the *co-mal,* the circular pottery griddle, over the fire. From Allan Richardson's superb photos of her performing, one can see that she struck the back of her right hand against the palm of her left—a conventional gesture of defiance. When she speaks in the Wasson velada of going on her "knees of tortillas, knees of water (*xco nio, xco nanta*)," her arms held out in imploration, it is illuminating to remember that she, like other women of her generation, was accustomed to grinding corn kernels as she knelt on the ground at the metate, pushing the pestle back and forth in her hands. *Chota nio, chota nanta,* the medicine man from Xochitonalco called human beings in his chants: "people of tortilla and water."

ROOT WOMAN

After chanting about roots, the medicine man from Xochitonalco asked me in Spanish if I knew who the *Chjon Lucia sen ngui nte* is: "the Woman Lucia under the earth." He explained that there is a woman lying under the earth who helps the plants grow. When she changes position, it causes earthquakes. The words of one shaman illuminate those of another. María Sabina invokes this same woman in the Folk-ways session without giving her a Catholic name: *Chonai Nataona sen ngui nte*—"Our Doll Virgin Beneath the Earth." In the Wasson velada she also associates her with roots. "Father, look, I have your staff of sap, your staff of the dew / Mother Patroness, look at how poor I am, at how humble I am / I am a poor woman, I am a humble woman / I am a green woman, I am a woman of clarity / I am a big root woman, I am a root woman beneath the water / I am a woman who branches out, I am a woman like a begonia / I go up to heaven, beneath your gaze, beneath your glory / There is my paper, there is my book / I am the Woman Beneath the Earth, I am the *chjon chjoa cama.*"

In the thought of all, the *chota chjine, jts?en*—"offshoot, branch"—goes together with *hama*—"root"—and is connected with the idea of children. The choices of words are determined by constraints inher-ent in the language, in its linkage of concepts. Different people prof-fer the same words because it is their language and culture speaking through them.

In both the Folkways session and the Wasson velada, María Sa-bina gives the Woman-Beneath-the-Earth the epithets *chjon cjoa cama, chjon xon ntijin*—appellatives that remain obscure. I have tenta-tively translated them as "woman for whom things multiply, woman paper blackened with smoke." They are old conjurer words nobody knows the meaning of anymore.

Evaristo G. Estrada, Álvaro's father and my father-in-law, a man of great sophistication in his culture, versed in the Mazatec language, once remarked to me, "Who knows where that little old lady gets her words from." She herself was reluctant to explain them. When Álvaro brought her to visit us one day in Mexico City, I took the opportunity to ask her through him and his sister what *na jncha ?no* means—the phrase translated as "big town woman," but which I conjecture is another atmospherical phenomenon used as a metaphor for the networks of light one sees, projected before one's eyes, on the mushrooms. "It's at the feet of Christ" is all she would say. In response to "Why do you speak of the path of the tracks of the feet?" the old woman replied, "We have our force in our feet," her toes splayed wide apart from years of walking barefoot over the earth.

CLOWN WOMAN

Many of the shamans call the mushrooms "clowns." When María Sabina calls herself a clown woman, it is an expression of her good humor and euphoric exuberance. She is not a funny clown. She is a *sase nai, sase chikon*—a "lord clown, sacred clown." She told Fernando Benítez, the Mexican writer and influential editor of cultural supplements in Mexico City newspapers, "I see the mushrooms like children, like clowns. Children with violins, children with trumpets, clown children who sing and dance around me." The idea of clowns points to the curative power of laughter, which is one of the characteristics of these emotional, cathartic experiences in which people laugh and cry. During the session, humming and clapping, calling out her host's name as if to bring him to himself, even before she calls herself a clown woman, there is humor in her voice and her listener is laughing with pleasure.

LAW WOMAN

When María Sabina says, "I know how to speak with the judge, the judge knows me," she is describing her role as an intermediary between the community and the supernatural. *Juez, gobierno, licenciada* are all said in Spanish. The lawyer is one who arranges a person's affairs with the law, and in her society, where sickness is considered to have not natural but spiritual causes and can often be the consequence of transgressions, that is precisely the function of the *chota chjine:* to intercede for the patient and argue his or her case with the powers that govern life.

A *chota chjine* long since deceased, whose words survive only in the memories of his listeners (who have also passed away) was remembered to have said, "I went to resolve things, I went to investigate where the table is, the brilliant table, the table of dew, where the law is, where the book of the law is. What motive is there? Who placed a complaint? Who whistled? Who shouted? From where comes this sickness, this suffering?" The theme of justice and the law in the chants of María Sabina is therefore not unique to her but a part of the traditional rhetoric of the Mazatec curers.

WARRIOR WOMAN

In her chants, María Sabina consistently associates the shooting star with San Pedro, the Mazatec deity of tobacco. Probably the connecting idea is fire. *Picietl*—"ground tobacco"—is considered a hot herb (the Maya in Yucatan believe shooting stars are the embers the rain gods flick from their cigars). From the beginning of the Wasson velada she felt beset by enemies. "Somebody is getting in the way," she says and asks for a cigarette to drive away the evil spirits, invoking San Pedro and San Pablo. That night, treating a sick boy, she clamors for justice. Over and over she tells her patient, "Don't be frightened. Perk up, perk up." Her enemies become his. "Justice, justice, justice. This woman of war, hunting dog woman. Lawyer woman. Transactions. Mexican flag. I'm more than a man." It is as if she were waving the flag in the front lines of battle. She becomes a hunting dog on the heels of the enemy. "I only throw out and scatter, says. Yes Jesus Christ, says. I am a woman general, says. I am a trumpet woman, says. I am a drum woman, says." Moments later: "I'm going to burn the world," she declares vehemently. "Yes Jesus Christ, says. I'm going to burn the world, says. Yes Jesus Christ, says. I am a shooting star woman, says. And woman San Pedro, says." The idea of setting the world on fire is a belligerent assertion of her devastating power against her enemies. "Didn't the woman of war win? Wasn't it the woman of war who won the most?" she asks, referring to the boy's enemies. In many Amerindian societies from the Arctic Circle to the Amazon, the shaman is thought to enter into battle with the forces of evil. "I'm going to doctor, I'm going to treat with herbs, this Christian. I'm going to lay my palms, I'm going to lay my hands on this Christian. I'm going to burn the world. Lawyer. Mexican flag. Benito Juárez. I'm more than a man." Her predecessors, the Nahuatl-speaking medicine men, in their conjurations to cure earache or pain in the jaw, after asking help from ground tobacco and "the children," chanted, "I came to destroy it, I came to burn it, I the priest, I the man of transformations." Often when she says, "I am going to demonstrate my courage," she invokes Benito Juárez—an Indian from Oaxaca like herself, the Mexican president who defeated the French. She alone of all the shamans I have heard introduces a historical person into her chants. Ironically, since Benito Juárez expropriated the property of the Catholic clergy and established a rigorous separation between Church and State, she gives the secular hero the status of a saint by invoking him together with the Virgin of Guadalupe and the Magdalene.

BOOK WOMAN

This "woman of good words, good breath, and good saliva," as she designates herself in her chants, whose own language is unwritten, is fascinated, obsessed by the idea of the book. She called herself a "Book Woman" long before she became the subject of books and articles, as if she were truly prophetic. The book plays a large part in the imagination of all the Mazatec *chota chjine,* either as a compendium of knowledge they receive like a diploma or as the register in which the destiny of people is written. The medicine man from Xochitonalco told me he once had a vision of Christ descending with a golden book, which he gave him. The red marker in the book meant that he was to be a deliverer of babies. The shaman from the Loma de Chapultepec, speaking of San Pedro, imagines him saying, "I will leave you a table and a book on it so that you can cure." The wise woman I recorded, whose sons are teachers, calls for a schoolbook in Castilian. But in the chants of María Sabina the theme of the book has a central place it does not have in the words of any of the other shamans.

She stands at the convergence of the religious traditions of Mesoamerica and Christianity. When she says in the velada, "It is your clean book, it is your clean quill, that I have, Father," she is probably thinking of the statue of San Juan Evangelista—the patron saint of Huautla—who stands in the church with a feather pen in one hand and a book in the other (today a scroll). The sources of the book in her imagination are the Bible from which the priest reads at mass in a language unintelligible to the barefoot faithful, and the municipal legal documents of the modern Mexican state on the margins of which she lived. At the same time her image of the book has antecedents in her autochthonous pre-Hispanic past: the *tonalamatl*—the "book of days" —in which the soothsayers read the fate of a child by the day sign of its birth, and the Mixtec histories painted on folded lengths of deerskin, in which the images march along in pairs like the couplets of her chants. Across five centuries, what is the connecting link between the picture books of ancient Mesoamerica and the book in the mind of a twentieth-century indigenous Oaxacan medicine woman? Continuous oral transmission is implausible. The collective unconscious is too hypothetical a notion. I think the connection has to be sought in the experience itself from which the image originates. The idea of writing may have been suggested to her by the manifestation of visual patterns characteristic of the psychedelic experience. People compare the abstract designs they see to the motifs of tapestries and oriental carpets. For María Sabina they must have at least once taken the form of script. She says the pages of the book were covered with letters.

The words of Netzahualcóyotl (1402–1472), the mystic poet and ruler of Texcoco, apply to her, probably the last great oral poet in the Mesoamerican religious tradition: "A book of paintings is your heart, / you have come to sing, / you make your drums resound, / you are the singer, / within the house of spring, / you make people happy. / You only distribute / flowers that intoxicate, / precious flowers, / you are the singer. / Within the house of spring, / you make people happy."

Three recorded ceremonies given by María Sabina over the course of fourteen years give us a chance to answer the question, Does she invent from session to session, saying whatever comes into her head on the inspiration of the moment, or does she always say the same thing, repeating herself over and over? The essential difference seems to be the emphasis she gives to her themes. In the 1958 velada, references to justice and law predominate, whereas in the ceremony twelve years later they are of minor importance in comparison with images of water. The presence of different people each time for whom it is necessary to speak is the major incentive for creative improvisation. Constant motifs enter into fresh combinations and are elaborated in different ways from night to night. The 1958 velada is the only night she calls herself a root woman, says she is a hunting dog woman, and declares she is a woman of war. But in general she invents little in comparison with the poet of the Western modern tradition who searches for new ideas and images. Her associations persist over the years as if they were written in her mind.

She gives the double parallel expressions of traditional Mesoamerican rhetoric a bilingual extension that reflects her social situation, her indigenous language encroached upon by the national language. When she says, "I have my paper, I have my book," she uses first the Mazatec word for book—*xon,* "paper"—then the word in Spanish, *libro.* She calls for *justicia,* then she translates the concept into Mazatec, *khoatexoma.* She is constantly code-switching back and forth. To call her a "monoglot Indian" is to underestimate her intelligence. She couldn't speak Spanish, but she knew many words in Spanish. She is what she calls herself: a woman wise in words, an interpreter woman. When she says, *Chjon chjine xqui nia, chjon chjine xca nia*—"I am a woman wise in medicine, I am a woman wise in herbs"—she often says in the next breath, *chjon* médico *nia*—"I am a doctor woman." In the Folkways session after saying, *ntia khoa ma, ntia khoa tao*—"the path of business, the path of recompense"—she translates it into Spanish, *ntia* trabajo—"the path of work."

The imagination overflows the limits of reality, and in her chants, as in her profession with the respect it commands, she transcends the inferior, subservient position imposed on women in traditional Mazatec society. In that sense this medicine woman and poet is a liberated woman. She is not only a mother woman, she is a lawyer woman, a woman general. When she says she is demonstrating her courage, what she says literally is, "I am going to demonstrate my manliness." Her bellicose assertion in Spanish, "Yo soy que más hombre" (*sic*), means not that she is superhuman but that she is more of a man than a man. Even the frequent affirmation in her chants that she is a trumpet woman, a drum woman, a woman violinist goes beyond the roles allotted to women by her society. In fact, I once overheard a man in Huautla saying to another that the fame of María Sabina puts into disrepute the wisdom of Mazatec men.

The couplet *chjon nca coya nia, chjon nca co t?a nia*—"I am a woman who looks into the insides of things, I am a woman who examines"—gives an idea of how her words go together in pairs not only because they complement each other in meaning but also because they sound similar. Toward the end of the Wasson velada, she proffers all her personae one after the other in a magnificent passage: *chjon tjotsin nia, chjon tjone nia, chjon tontso?o nia, chjon nca tontsin nia*—"I am a woman who resounds, I am a woman torn up (out of the ground), I am a spider woman, I am a hummingbird woman." The euphony of her chants is based not on rhyme but on the consonance between words.

The session is a praxis of language with a therapeutic aim. *Tixai, tixai*—"Work, work"—her listeners tell her, urging her on in the same spirit that people listening to jazz yell out enthusiastically, "Tell it like it is." Expression is exertion. She says to the sick boy, "Perk up, perk up," clapping her hands to bring him to life. The shaman has to keep in touch with her or his patients, guide them, protect them, talk for them, drive the sickness out of them. The greatest praise anyone can give a shaman is to say she or he "trabaja bonita": works well. When she says something particularly beautiful, the listeners spontaneously exclaim, *Naskata chili*—"Thank you."

At the end of the Wasson velada, after calling herself a "woman whirlpool in the lake, a woman who sees into the insides of things," she says, "I go down underneath the ground, says / Yes Jesus Christ, says / My words join Word Rock." *Lao en,* Word Rock, is the native name of the town of Quiotepec in the Cañada Oaxaqueña where the

Río Grande from Oaxaca joins the Río Salado from the Valley of Tehuacán to become the Río Santo Domingo that enters the mountains in a deep canyon. The Mazatecs call it *Nta he,* the Big Water, but they also give it an esoteric name: *Nta en,* the River of Words. It is as if she imagines what she says going down into the ground like the water of the rain into sinkholes, to flow through some of the deepest caves in the world until it comes out into the river far away below, as for centuries the words of innumerable shamans singing in the night have entered a great stream of language running from generation to generation.

In the chants of María Sabina, we can appreciate the interplay of individual invention and traditional liturgy within the oral creativity of a nonliterate society. The recordings of her words that have saved them from oblivion give us the opportunity to glimpse the emergence of a genius from the soil of the communal, religious folk poetry of a native Mexican campesino people.

SOURCES

For the Mazatec language, the basic texts are Eunice V. Pike, "Huautla de Jiménez Mazatec," in *Handbook of Middle American Indians,* volume 5, edited by Robert Wauchope (Austin: University of Texas Press, 1967); and George M. Cowan, "The Mazatec Language," in R. Gordon Wasson et al., *María Sabina and Her Mazatec Mushroom Velada* (New York and London: Harcourt Brace Jovanovich, 1974). My writing of the Mazatec words is based on George and Florence Cowan's transcription of the 1958 velada in the latter book and on Eunice V. Pike's *Vocabulario mazateco* (Mexico: Instituto Lingüístico de Verano, 1952).

For material on Huautla, see the chapter "Huauhtla [*sic*] and the Mazatecs (1900)" in Frederick Starr's *In Indian Mexico* (Chicago: Forbes & Co., 1908), a delightful, insightful look at what he calls "this great Indian town." Carlos Incháustegui, the first director of the Instituto Nacional Indigenista in Huautla, has written an important trilogy on Mazatec myths and beliefs: *Relatos del mundo mágico mazateco* (Mexico: Centro Regional Puebla-Tlaxcala, Instituto Nacional de Antropología e Historia, 1977), *Figuras en la niebla: relatos y creencias de los mazatecos* (Tlahuapán, Puebla: Red de Jonas/Cultura Popular, Premia Editora, 1983), and *La mesa de plata: cosmogonía y curanderismo entre los mazatecos de Oaxaca* (Mexico: Instituto Oaxaqueño de las Culturas, 1994). The opossum myth and the reference to God being on the other side of the ocean are taken from the first of these.

The first book in Spanish about María Sabina was *Los hongos alucinantes* by Fernando Benítez, included in volume three of his five-volume work, *Los indios de México* (Mexico: Ediciones Era, 1964, 1970).

On historical background: Dr. Alfonso Caso first identified the shamanic session depicted in the *Codex Vindobonensis obverse*. See his "Representaciones de hongos en los códices," *Estudios de cultura náhuatl* 4 (1963). Quotations from Fray Bernardino de Sahagún's *Historia general de las cosas de Nueva España* are from the Angel María Garibay edition (Mexico: Editorial Porrua, 1956). The poem by Netzahualcóyotl is from Miguel León-Portilla's translation in his *Trece poetas del mundo azteca* (Mexico: Universidad Nacional Autónoma de México, Instituto de Investigaciones Históricas, 1967). For translations of the conjurations collected by the priest Hernando Ruiz de Alarcón in the seventeenth century, see Alfredo López Austin, "Conjuros médicos de los nahuas," *Revista de la Universidad de México* (July 1970).

MARÍA SABINA IN MEXICO CITY

HOMERO ARIDJIS

A native of Contepec, Michoacán, Homero Aridjis came early to Mexico City, building from there a life as poet, novelist, editor, and sometime diplomat, more recently (through the Group of One Hundred, founded by him and Betty Ferber Aridjis) as spokesman for endangered species (animals and humans; ecosystems and deep cultures). Over the years he has become a major presence in Latin American and world poetry, of whom Kenneth Rexroth wrote, "I can think of no poet of Aridjis' generation in the Western Hemisphere who is as much at ease in the blue spaces of illumination." He served from 1997 to 2003 as the president of PEN International, in which position he was able to advance an agenda centered on the relation of poetry to questions of ecological and cultural diversity. In a mode derived from pre-Conquest and later indigenous sources he writes: "I dream of seeing the face of the earth / mother of beings and mother of my mother / and the face of heaven / father of air and father of my father / now / its shadow appears in my mouth / its fire in my eyes / carried by time / my body   sacred / trembles" (translated by Eliot Weinberger).

One February day in 1983 my wife Betty and I were driving down Avenida de Las Palmas in Mexico City when we suddenly saw a head-line in an afternoon newspaper saying that María Sabina was sick. We bought the paper and read that one of the best poets, not only of Mexico but of the entire American continent, was dying in poverty.

Then I remembered R. Gordon Wasson's words about Sabina: "Who knows? Perhaps María Sabina bids fair to become the most famous Mexican of her time. Long after the personages of contemporary Mexico sink back into the forgotten slough of the dead past, her name and what she stood for may remain etched in men's minds."

R. Gordon Wasson was right in saying this. He had experienced the magic powers of the "wise woman of the mushrooms" on the night of June 12, 1958, when she held a *velada* with the little *saint children,* a hallucinogenic mushroom ritual, to cure Perfecto José García, a seventeen-year-old boy, who was seriously ill. That night the mushroom sang, "There is no cure now." Then six weeks later Perfecto died.

Given that this assessment was written by Wasson, a foreigner, the historians of our Hispanic culture were not about to give it any credence. Besides, many of our literary critics, followers of fashionable Western letters, have ignored the figure and work of María Sabina, even after her death. She was an Indian poet who sang her poems in the Mazatec tongue. Her chants were first translated from English to Spanish, not from Mazatec. None of our literati know this language and few even mention her. This is one of the forms that our cultural discrimination against the Indian world takes. And an ignorance of this world among Spanish speakers is something that can be readily seen, say, if one reads the poem that the Spanish writer and 1989 Nobel Prize winner Camilio José Cela dedicated to her. This poem is one of the most absurd and nonsensical texts that any human being has stitched together in the twentieth century.

I contacted the newspaper to send a message to her through their reporter. To my surprise I received a collect long-distance call the next day from Oaxaca. It was her grand-nephew Juan García Carrera, who told me that he was bringing María Sabina by taxi from Huautla de Jiménez to Mexico City so that I could help her.

So, when they arrived in the Distrito Federal, Betty and I went to pick them up (María Sabina and three companions) at the Tapo Bus Station, because the cab driver didn't want to go farther than Puebla.

We had made arrangements for her at the National Institute of Cardiology, and at about eleven P.M. María Sabina was examined by the doctors. It wasn't necessary to hospitalize her, so we took them all to a hotel where they stayed that night and the following days.

In the meantime, a journalist attacked me in a Mexico City newspaper, since he had gone to Huautla de Jiménez to interview her, only to find out that she had come to the capital to see me.

Then, thanks to the help of Dr. Cristina León, who had known her for some time before, she was taken to the General Hospital. But when they arrived there, her relatives called me again, telling me that she hadn't been admitted. She was an Indian and so she needed to have an identity card from the Mexican National Peasants Confederation of the Institutional Revolutionary Party (PRI), and she not only didn't have one but had no idea what they were talking about. Finally she was admitted.

When the other patients became aware of her presence, they sought her out in her room in the hope that she would cure them. And not only patients came to consult her, but even some doctors and nurses who suffered from certain serious illnesses that Western medicine couldn't cure.

On one of those days a reporter from Televisa TV put a microphone in front of her and asked her why she couldn't cure herself if she was such a *curandera*. María Sabina answered him that she couldn't in fact cure herself of old age and poverty.

In statements that she made for the Mexican daily *Excélsior* the night of her arrival, María Sabina complained that "the government has always denied help for the poor, even more for the Indians. Before

I die I would like to see my people get help. This is one of my dreams, to see that other Indians like me are rescued from their misery."

Those words now seem more timely than ever, like the conversations we had in my home around that time and which I have finally decided to publish. My perspective on her has not changed since then. I still think she is one of the greatest Mexican poets of the twentieth century and a great shaman. Her language is still present in my mind, different from the one we Mexicans use in our daily lives—that magic language she heard for the first time when she was between five and seven years old and the wise man Juan Manuel came to cure her uncle Emilio Cristino. (See above, page 11.)

After this experience, she would come to revelations of her own through the mushrooms: "They were the same mushrooms that the Wise Man Juan Manuel had eaten. I knew them well. My hands gently tore up one mushroom, then another. I looked at them up close. 'If I eat you, you, and you,' I said to them, 'I know that you will make me sing beautifully.'"

The initiation into the world of ecstasy came to María Sabina in the midst of the terrible poverty in which she and her sister lived, that Indian poverty that accompanied her throughout her life, oscillating between physical hunger and spiritual insight. . . . Through the mushrooms María Sabina learned to see and talk with the dead, and she kept eating them until she realized that "the mushrooms were like God."

As a sign of gratitude for what Betty and I did for her, María Sabina gave us a copy of her *Vida* signed with her thumbprint. She didn't know how to read or write. She never went to school, nor did she learn to speak Spanish. Her parents spoke only Mazatec. Although she confessed that she didn't know what a school was or even if one existed, "if there had been a school, I wouldn't have gone, because there wasn't time. In those days, people worked a lot," making tortillas and doing domestic chores, she tells us in her *Vida*.

As a twenty-year-old widow of someone called Serapio, and with three children, María Sabina continued a life of hunger and poverty; she supported herself working the soil and cutting wood, planting beans, picking corn, and harvesting coffee.

María Sabina would later cure her sister by eating mushrooms. While she was curing her, the Mazatec seer—like Hildegard of Bingen, the sibyl of the Rhine—had a vision: "Some people appeared who inspired me with respect. I knew they were the Principal Ones of whom my ancestors spoke. They were seated behind a table on which there were many written papers.... On the Principal Ones' table a book appeared, an open book that went on growing until it was the size of a person.... One of the Principal Ones spoke to me and said: 'María Sabina, this is the Book of Wisdom. It is the Book of Language. Everything that is written in it is for you. The Book is yours, take it so that you can work.' I exclaimed with emotion: 'That is for me. I receive it.'"

"I had attained perfection," María Sabina tells us, "I was no longer a simple apprentice." And during that same midnight *velada,* after having had two visions—in one of which the Supreme Lord of the Mountains, Chicon Nindó, came to her riding a white horse, and in the second one a kind of god of vegetation—María Sabina, besides curing her sister, discovered the Language of God: "Language makes the dying return to life. The sick recover their health when they hear the words taught by the *saint children.* There is no mortal who can teach this Language."

María Sabina gave Betty and me a gift of coffee and a cloth she had embroidered with mushrooms, and she indicated to us that she didn't want to do any more trips, because she was afraid that she wouldn't return from them and because so much strength was needed to take the mushrooms, but she would be more than willing to do it for us. We couldn't go to Huautla to do the trip with her. But even now the temptation of that lost vision haunts us—especially me, who never took mushrooms or any drug, although as a young poet myself I knew the Beat poets who came down to Mexico in the late fifties and the beginning of the sixties searching for the beatific, and many times drugs were made available to us at literary parties.

María Sabina returned to Huautla de Jiménez and died on November 22, 1985, maybe at the age of ninety-seven (nobody ever knew her real age). It wasn't known precisely when she was born. Even she herself wasn't sure: "I don't know in what year I was born, but my mother, María Concepción, told me that it was in the morning of the day they celebrate the Virgin Magdalene, there in Río Santiago, an *agencia* in the municipality of Huautla. None of my ancestors knew their age."

In a brief communiqué, the doctor Derna Nila Nodales reported that "her age, pernicious anemia, pulmonary emphysema, advanced malnutrition, chronic bronchitis, and nose bleeding were the causes of the death of the Mazatec woman."

"The kingdom of the dead is silent, dark and warm ... there is no coldness there ... there is no need for fear, one must be close to the dead, we are closer to them than to the living who swindle and cheat us," María Sabina declared before dying. "I don't see my face, I don't see it. I see peace in that world, and yet I feel sad. I see people whom I knew in my childhood: my grandfather, my great-grandfather, and my parents."

At dawn, in her house (where the *velada* took place), after the cock crowed it was passed over her stiff body. From the sierra dozens of Indians came down to accompany her on the way to the town cemetery. According to the Mazatec ritual, her soul was received in heaven by San Pedro.

Translation from Spanish by
Laura Jáuregui and Heriberto Yépez

from FAST SPEAKING WOMAN

ANNE WALDMAN

Anne Waldman has been a force in United States poetry since the early 1960s—
as a poet foremost but with a lifetime involvement as well in creating and caring
for poetic communities. After heading the St. Mark's Church Poetry Project in
New York, she founded with Allen Ginsberg and continues to direct the Jack Kerouac
School of Disembodied Poetics at the Buddhist-centered Naropa University in Boulder,
Colorado. This commitment to poetry and community (in particular to what she
speaks of, wisely, as "the outrider tradition") has led to her experimental work as a
performer and to her exploration of "chant" as central to contemporary performance
poetry. Her own long chant-poem, Fast Speaking Woman *(1975), emerged from*
an introduction to the recorded texts of María Sabina, an example of ethnopoetic
structures impacting new poetic works over great cultural distances.

> *"I is another"* — RIMBAUD

because I don't have spit
because I don't have rubbish
because I don't have dust
because I don't have that which is in air
because I am air
let me try you with my magic power

I'm a shouting woman
I'm a speech woman

I'm an atmosphere woman
I'm an airtight woman
I'm a flesh woman
I'm a flexible woman
I'm a high-heeled woman
I'm a high-style woman
I'm an automobile woman
I'm a mobile woman
I'm an elastic woman
I'm a necklace woman
I'm a silk-scarf woman
I'm a know-nothing woman
I'm a know-it-all woman
I'm a day woman
I'm a doll woman
I'm a sun woman
I'm a late-afternoon woman
I'm a clock woman
I'm a wind woman
I'm a white woman
I'M A SILVER-LIGHT WOMAN
I'M AN AMBER-LIGHT WOMAN
I'M AN EMERALD-LIGHT WOMAN

I'm an abalone woman
I'm an abandoned woman
I'm the woman abashed, the gibberish woman
the aborigine woman, the woman absconding
the Nubian Woman
the antediluvian woman
the absent woman

the transparent woman
the absinthe woman
the woman absorbed, the woman under tyranny
the contemporary woman, the mocking woman
the artist dreaming inside her house

I'm the gadget woman
I'm the druid woman
I'm the Ibo woman
I'm the Yoruba woman
I'm the vibrato woman
I'm the rippling woman
I'm the gutted woman
I'm the woman without wounds
I'm the woman with shins
I'm the bruised woman
I'm the eroding woman
I'm the suspended woman
I'm the woman alluring
I'm the architect woman
I'm the trout woman
I'm the tungsten woman
I'm the woman with the keys
I'm the woman with the glue

I'm a fast speaking woman

> water that cleans
> flowers that clean
> water that cleans as I go

FAST SPEAKING WOMAN & THE DAKINI PRINCIPLE

ANNE WALDMAN

Wisdom is Language. —MARÍA SABINA

As I began writing *Fast Speaking Woman,* I had in my head that I would do a list-chant naming all the kinds of women there are to be, interweaving personal details (how I configure the biographical self: "I'm the impatient woman," "The woman with the keys") with all the energetic adjectives I could conjure up to make the chant speak of/to/for "everywoman." Chant is heartbeat. Chant in all cultures is ancient efficacious poetic practice. One of the oldest pre-Christian lyrics is the gnomic Song of Amergin, a Celtic calendar-alphabet, found in various Irish and Welsh variants, which has such lines as:

I am a stag: of seven tines,
I am a flood: across a plain,
I am a wind: on a deep lake,
I am a tear: the Sun lets fall,
I am a hawk: above a cliff,
I am a thorn: beneath the nail,
I am a wonder: among flowers
I am a wizard: who but I
Sets the cool head aflame with smoke?

This also resembles the Welsh Cad Goddeu or "The Battle of the Trees" with its ubiquitous litany:

I have been a drop in the air.
I have been a shining star.
I have been a word in a book.
I have been a book originally.
I have been a light in a lantern.

I wanted to use this elemental modal structure to capture Everywoman's psyche. The "bottom nature," Gertrude Stein calls it, of any human. I enjoyed the bold equation of human "I" identity being at one with animal, word, lantern. Now it would be omnipresent with "woman." Timely, for there was an unprecedented wave of strong writers and artists coming to the fore on the American cultural landscape, who happened to be women. Any woman might be thinking, imagining, hearing and saying the same things I was to "name."

Fast Speaking Woman began on a trip to South America in 1972, a voyage that triggered durable interest in Meso-American and South American tantra. "Tantra" literally means "continuity" in the Tibetan Buddhist sense and refers to the continuity through the ground, path and fruition of a spiritual journey. Continuity of ground remains "like the sky." Continuity of path means you apply exertion (through practice) to overcome aggression, greed, ignorance. Fruition tantra means you join the wisdom of the teachings and the teachers to your life. Thus, continuity: the ground has been there from the beginning. Tantra is referred to as an unbroken golden thread.

I was studying these things hard. Tantra also relates to the quick path of practice, or Vajrayana, whereby initiates work to overcome basic "ego"—basic grasping, attachment in this lifetime. It's often a radical shift, requiring extreme measures. The suffering that humans

—these "hairy bags of water"—carry and perpetuate onto others urgently needs to be revoked. Powerful demonic visualizations are conjured. Images of rotting corpses, skull cups of blood, wrathful deities of all horrific description haunt and vivify the premises. Death is the magnificent teacher that wakes you up. Mantras are sung to recognize and invite the provocative, transformative energies into the very specific human realm of chaos and desire and ignorance. Poetry always seemed an aspect of the spiritual path. Tibetan Vajrayana clearly draws on the pre-Buddhist shamanic practices of Tibet. Dakinis (Tibetan: *mkha'-'gro-ma*) are female tricksters, energy principles that roam charnel grounds, engage in the play between samsara and nirvana moment to moment. They inspire the union of *upaya* (skillful means) and *prajna* (wisdom).

Applied in the indigenous American context, tantra might refer to the unequivocal power, energy, magic and healing properties of human mind and sacred language, and the unbroken continuity of enlightenment or "seeing." The fierce images, the "states of mind" one perceives in Olmec, Toltec, Aztec, Maya iconography are not unlike the fierce shamanic deities of Tibetan Buddhism. The legends and myths handed down, cosmologies rampant with visionary landscapes, magical animal doings, bloody battles, and dramatic couplings resonate with many other "wisdom traditions" as well.

I wrote down a list with all the "A" words in a notebook beginning with "I'm an abalone woman" to "the artist dreaming inside her house." I wanted to assert the sense of my mind, my imagination being able to travel as artist, as maker, as inventor. To see beyond false boundaries. As Essie Parrish, a Pomo shaman, has said: "I don't have to go nowhere to see. / Visions are everywhere." And yet I needed to travel. The poem was written at the Alto de los Ídolos in Colombia; in Secua, Ecuador; in Machu Picchu; at home on St. Mark's Place in

New York City. The chant seemed to fall into distinct sections with more sound associations than anything else mnemonic; thus "d": "defiant," "demented," "demi-monde"; "s": "solo," "sapphire," "stay-at-home." Obviously, "butterfly" counters "stay-at-home." Like that. Very simple, quick—almost child-like—associations, letting the drive of the repeating assertions take over. Naming, that was the thrust. And the chant was to be spoken. Or sung. Or more interestingly, *sprechstimme,* spoke-sung.

I was downtown-white-New York-young-sophisticate college-graduate-bohemian, but real poet too, reading books, writing books, listening to jazz, dabbling in psychotropic drugs, magics, beginning an apprenticeship in tantric Buddhism, attracted to shamanic energies and pulses of all kinds. I had taken preliminary "refuge" vows in the Tibetan Buddhist tradition. I had traveled in various exotic directions and was already "poet" with published work, and Director of the very oral-based Poetry Project at St. Mark's Church-in-the-Bowery. By the late sixties I was reading my poems aloud a good deal, involved with the activities of Giorno Poetry Systems, helping edit the Dial-A-Poem series, protesting the war in Vietnam, presenting work collaboratively with other artists and musicians, improvising into tape recorders, editing magazines and anthologies.

I was neither a shaman nor a psychic healer. No special pleading here. I made no claims beyond those of word/cultural-worker. I was a "product" to some extent of my generation, the culture, the radical (were they? in poetry certainly, in politics, in Buddhism) times, but when I meditated or took mushrooms or ingested peyote, or hiked the Andes and Himalayas or read deep in Blake or Shakespeare or tried to imitate Navajo chant off recordings—not to co-opt it but to taste it—I was timeless seeker in my own imagination's interstices, passionately in love with the magics of the phenomenal world. I also took

Gertrude Stein's language to heart as mentor, as guide. She was out-rageous.

Comrade-poet Michael Brownstein with whom I'd traveled south brought me the Folkways recording of *Mushroom Ceremony of the Mazatec Indians of Mexico,* which had been recorded the night of July 21–22, 1956, by V. P. and R. Gordon Wasson. It included Sabina's text translated from Mazatec into Spanish and English. My friend knew I would be gripped by it, and could "use" it, appropriating shame-lessly, as poets are wont to do. Fired by Sabina's potent voice (both the sound and the sense, in translation), I then interwove some of her lines and picked up on the refrain "water that cleans as I go," also us-ing it as a place to pause and shift rhythm and acknowledge the cleans-ing impulse of the writing. Although the soundings—Sabina's voice chanting—are very different, the text as transcribed into English clicked with my young woman poem's thrust and intention. A woman list. And declaration of power through accretion/repetition. Efficacy through language.

R. Gordon Wasson, in his "Retrospective Essay" that introduces the original English version (1981) of Álvaro Estrada's transcription and arrangement of María Sabina's *Vida,* speaks of how, in discussing the similarities between the Nahuatl and Mazatec "veladas," María Sabina and the Nahuatl Wise One "engage in an elaborate self-pres-entation, beginning in María Sabina's case with professions of humil-ity and working up to assertions of power and even ability to talk with the supernatural beings almost on terms of equality." Her renderings, compared to mine, come out of pure vision and purpose and include the sacred mushrooms speaking through her, the occasion of ritual ceremony, the underpinnings of tribal ritual overlaid with Christian litany. As such her "workings" (the voices of the mushrooms) are litanies of fully actualized authority. She travels through myriad realms, becoming omniscient, clairvoyant. Like the highly realized adepts in Tibetan Buddhism her consciousness discloses its power in many directions simultaneously. "She" is in all the corners of the universe. Her body of chants (as transcribed and in translation) is clearly one of the great transformational language texts of any time.

My own composition, pale by comparison, is exploratory—resembling Gertrude Stein's "Lifting Belly"—impulsive, free associative, naive at times. I didn't want to draw on Sabina literally or faithfully, I wanted to absorb the experience of her works (in translation) in me, and put myself into her and then let the "text" (meant to be performed or sung) emerge as a kind of intuitive "re-working." The rhythms on her recording of course are entirely different from the translation, and from my own lines, but there is the overall sense of a journey, of continuous energy (sound in space) in act of traveling.

Often in early public readings I would add or improvise lines for the particular situation at hand. Once during a reading for the "street people" of Boulder, Colorado, in 1974, where organizers hadn't secured the proper permit for the public gathering, I saw two cops approaching from the distance. As they closed in I ascertained that they were both women. I immediately sprung to "I'm the blue cop woman," "I'm the woman with the billy club," "I'm the powerful bust-cop-lady assigned to close this reading down," and so on. The tension dispelled, the event continued. When I was chanting the poem for a scene in Bob Dylan's film *Renaldo and Clara* at Niagara Falls, dressed like a postcard American Indian (not my idea), I had to shout over the thundering waterfall, improvising lines that related to the situation: "I'm the deep-plunging-water-microphoned-thunder woman," etcetera. (This scene, mercifully, was not used in the movie, although some of the soundtrack of the poem accompanied shots of Dylan walking down a street, as if it's a "voice" in his head.)

I only knew of María Sabina through the Folkways recording when I wrote *Fast Speaking Woman.* Jerome Rothenberg told me more about her, and in 1976, Sara Dylan described her visit to Sabina and participation in a "velada" (vigil) and gave me a photograph of her. (By then, it was fashionable to make the trip to Huautla in Mexico to imbibe the *hongos.*) The Álvaro Estrada *Vida,* which I came on later, is both an invaluable ethnographic text and a heartbreaking account of the adulteration of a sacred practice. Estrada's transcription of Sabina's own explication of her difficult life and her coming to the *saint children,* along with the subsequent karma that resulted after her practices became publicized and abused, is a document for these dark times. María Sabina said, before her death, "From the moment the foreigners arrived, the *saint children* lost their purity. They lost their force; the foreigners spoiled them."

What survives, fortunately, is the poetry, which has a curative power. It is a kind of *"terma"*—or found wisdom treasure, a rune that needed unlocking—that Sabina brought to consciousness to benefit others. Perhaps the efficacy will be reclaimed in the future. She herself speaks of the power of Language to heal:

> Language makes the dying return to life. The sick recover their health when they hear the words taught by the *saint children.* I cure with Language, the Language of the *saint children.* When they advise me to sacrifice chickens, they are placed on the parts where it hurts. The rest is Language.
>
> ■
>
> Language belongs to the *saint children.* They speak and I have the power to translate. If I say that I am the little woman of the Book, that means that a Little-One-Who-Springs-Forth is a woman and that she

is the little woman of the Book. In that way, during the vigil, I turn into a mushroom—little woman—of the book....

If I am on the aquatic shore, I say:
I am a woman who is standing in the sand ...

Because wisdom comes from the place where the sand is born.

Since the first publication of *Fast Speaking Woman,* I've taught classes on shamanic and ethnopoetic literatures at the Naropa Institute, using, among other texts, Jerome Rothenberg's *Technicians of the Sacred,* as well as Sabina's imaginative chants. The class one year experimented with various ritual word-enactments to create a force field of energy for protest demonstrations at Rocky Flats plutonium plant in Boulder. One evolved into an anti-nuclear piece which was subsequently performed as a group collaboration. I also began chanting "Mega mega mega mega mega mega mega death bomb—ENLIGHTEN!" the summer of 1978 and a list of "glowings" ("teeth glowing," "microfilm glowing," "pages of words glowing"), later working the lines into the lyrics for a "new wave" recording of a piece entitled "Uh Oh Plutonium!"

In some respects of course the whole shaman concept is problematic. Lecturing in Munich some years ago on "the poet as shaman" and the difficult issues that artistic shamanism or even "white" shamanism raise—considering the hardships and trials of actual shaman practitioners—I wanted to make a case for the influence of shamanism in the work of specific writers and artists—Joseph Beuys being just one example. Poets are hardly shamans, a contentious critic exclaimed. They're jet-setters, bunglers, indulgent ego-maniacs. No doubt, I retorted—poets don't claim to be enlightened healers, but sometimes, because they're available as "antennae of the race," they can receive or tap into energy sources someone else might be deaf or impervious to.

They have a way with the Language. It is a calling, much like that of María Sabina. Whatever else she was, she was also a Poet.

I remember the delight I had when I began *Fast Speaking Woman,* thinking every woman can do this, every woman *is* doing this. Like the "dakini" principle in Buddhism, where every woman is a dakini or sky-walker, one who does not have to walk on the ground, who can travel and can reconfigure the world through the play of her imagination. She is both messenger and protector, embodying the qualities of compassion, emptiness, and wisdom.

THE LITTLE SAINT OF HUAUTLA

JEROME ROTHENBERG

I met María Sabina in 1979, brought to Huautla by Henry Munn and accompanied throughout by him and his wife Nati, the sister of Álvaro Estrada. The town was then remote—as it no longer is—and situated in the high mountains of the Mazatecan Sierras. But it was also clearly a part of our contemporary world, and even María Sabina's hillside house—across the path from the mobile home the government had put in place for her—had familiar objects in it that linked her world to ours. Her household altar—memorably—was the repository for what one took to be gifts brought there by two decades of foreign visitors. In memory I can still see vividly the images of Hindu gods that stood out from among the other, largely Catholic figures. She smoked packaged cigarettes—as we did—and offered us bottled beer too, but our presence was, I thought, of little interest to her. And when Henry Munn asked me—against my own judgment—to take a rattle and sing an American Indian song for her (in my translation), she listened for less than a minute and went off to attend to a crying grandchild or great-grandchild outside her door.

That was all as it should be and a clear indication of the one-sidedness of such a cultural meeting. It was also at Henry's suggestion, but possibly as her own idea, that she offered to arrange a velada for us—

for a price that she then named. That struck me as curious, since I had been reading in her *Vida,* which I was then helping to publish in English, that "a Wise One should not charge for her services" and that "one is born to cure, not to do business with her knowledge." At that moment too I realized, as never before, our mutual contemporaneity and the fate we shared as poets in an imperfect world.

The poem I wrote about that follows.

THE LITTLE SAINT OF HUAUTLA

lives to be too old
her voice
painful to her chest
echoes
until her belly sags
cries to the tumor
under her heart:
"o you moon child
"you little eye of god
"little birds that grow
"from trees
the drunk beside us
—young man
sans teeth—
who stumbles
to reach her hilltop
sits by the saint
& hiccups
"are you a saint?" he asks
"I am a governor" she tells him

"I am a clock
"a wheel
"the palsy in the judge's fingers
"flutters my skirts
"I am the moon
"I welcome my dizziness
"I chew the little things
"& whistle
"you will eat your eyes
"—the clock says—
"your shadows
"will slide down your throats
"will choke you
"you will come back to my hillside
"flying   martyrs
"will bang tibetan bells
"the mountain god
"little king on horseback
"will cut you down
the saint says
hides behind her lost teeth
the face of Krishna
smiles back at us
her own face in a glow
of cigarette smoke
as we make
small talk
small mirrors shine from
the robes of all saints
Mexico in summer

still wet with fruit
the garbage of poor lives
poor women know
their huipils bright with birds
& butterflies
flowers of the orange dance
—o mystic weddings—
where in Huautla de Jiménez
we were the last to come
the bus still bringing
freaks from Mexico
to eat the sour mushrooms
with earth & goat shit
wild on their lips:
this is language
tiny letters
so brilliant in the sky
of *la sierra mazateca*
where we arrive
to meet our tiger shamans
looking for their tracks
their footprints
like whirlwinds in far cities
torn from the earth
o clocks
o eagles
for you the sweat of Christ
Christ's semen
becomes a plant
transparent flower

glowing in ocean
someone walking with
Christ's flower
as a staff   a man
with money like a saint
general whose footprints leave
whole jewels
in our path
—she sings
searches for the night—
the drunk Indian
(poor boy)
smiles to her face
& hiccups
like a drum
his language dying in him
"are you a movie star?" he asks
"I am a calendar" she tells him
"I am a comet woman
"an opossum
"I drink warm beer
"freshly I make my bed
"my photographs envelop Mexico
"I cackle like a turkey
"my voice is endless
"in museums where shawls are hanging
"in bars in fancy homes in ballrooms
"in concert with the grateful dead
"France awaits me
"the Italian directors come at night

"they suck my mushrooms
"the Pope comes to Oaxaca with the others
"butlers are dancing with
"the brides of god
"brides of mountain men
"little kings on horseback
"Shiva's ikon dances
"on my altar
"clocks are dancing
"& opossums
"wheels & governors
"in dreams without a word
"left to intone
she says   it says
for her
the book of language says translated into broken Spanish
sold to feed the dead
the dying language
hiding from strangers' eyes
the way the mushrooms hide
will not speak
except when the children's voices
tell us:
casa
dinero
hongos
hidden from your eyes too
María poet of these hills
fast speaking woman
bought & sold

to feed the language of the rich
—cloaca of all languages—
—oppressors whom you love—
you hilltop woman
you saint woman
you clock woman
you moon woman
you martyr woman
you mirror woman
you tiger woman
you language woman
you flower woman
you money woman
you warm beer woman
you my mother shepherdess
(it says)
o mother of the sap (it says)
mother of the dew (it says)
mother of breasts (it says)
mother of the harvest
you rich mother
now standing visible & loud
before us
ha ha ha
so so so
so so so
hee hee hee
see see see
hum hum hum
it says & rises

lonely   lost
the spirit that wanders through America
saint children
disembodied in city air
crazy in Mexico
a squatters' village to hold the poor
fury of dead Mazatecs
the ghost of Juárez
speaking English
like my own voice
at your doorway
shaking this sad rattle
singing
without the hope of god
or clocks
with no word between us
veladas that cost
a thousand pesos
this vigil for your book
& mine
for any languages
still left to sell

THE POET SPEAKS,
THE MOUNTAIN SINGS …

JUAN GREGORIO REGINO

Since the late 1970s Juan Gregorio Regino has been a leading figure in the movement
— throughout Latin America — aimed at the creation of new literatures using native
languages alongside the dominant Spanish. A Mazatec by birth and upbringing,
Regino was a cofounder and president of the Comité Directivo de Escritores en
Lenguas Indígenas (Association of Indigenous Writers). His poetry and other
writings have appeared in his own Mazatec and Spanish versions, and in 1996
he received the Netzahualcóyotl Prize for Indigenous Literature. The remarks that
follow were made in response to this award, an example of the continuities between
the Mazatec past and a present shared with oral poets such as María Sabina.

K'e tjien fucho ena.	*Up to here my voice can be heard.*
K'e tjien fucho ndana.	*Up to here my spirit extends.*
Kui ndi'ya xi tsja tjik'ien.	*In this house that gives shade.*
Kui ndi'ya xi tsja isien.	*In this house that refreshes.*

Our writing was interrupted many years ago, and yet we have learned
by means of orality to preserve our memory. From the people of wis-
dom in my land I have learned to value and to cultivate the word.
For my people the word is truth, feeling, memory, symbol of struggle,
of resistance, of identity. To possess it and to re-create it is a way of
knowledge, a form of communion with the sacred, a pact with nature,
a romance with the universe. In the dense vegetation of our moun-

tains, it is not only the poet who speaks; the mountain sings also, the duendes of the ceiba also raise their voices, the duendes of the blue cascades, the duendes of the deep ravines. The countryside is also poetry; woman is also.

To make indigenous literature is neither folklore nor a passing fashion; it is a dialogue of identities, of civilizations, of languages, of millenarian voices and perennial spirits.

It is fellowship, it is respect for difference, it is the knowledge of one for the other.

The indigenous languages are a patrimony of our country that should not go on developing in hiding and subordination. They are living languages whose contact with Spanish brings a mutual enrichment, because there are no pure languages and no superior or inferior ones.

Our peoples have not remained static, they construct their truth every day; today we can say that we sing in two voices, we whistle in two tongues. We believe in the language of the earth we have cultivated, we believe in the language that arrived from the other side of the ocean, we believe in the universal language of the sun. Languages are our treasures as our identity is the eagle and the serpent, the crowns and the laurels.

We have survived ethnocide, we have learned to write and to cultivate our minds with foreign books. Today we are recovering the tradition of the tlacuilos, blanketed beneath a single concept: Mexico. Today is a time of unity, of peace and of work.

I am ending my presentation with a fragment of the words of a great Mazatec woman: María Sabina.

Ngat'e xujun Né.	Because they are the papers of the judge
K'ui xujun kjuakjintakun.	It is the Book of your law

K'ui xujun xtitjun.	It is the Book of your government
Ngat'e mana chjajo 'an jaa	Because I know how to speak with your eagle
Ngaté béjne ngasundie.	Because the world knows us
Ngat'e béjne Néna.	Because God knows us

Translation from Spanish by
Jerome Rothenberg

THE SONG BEGINS

JUAN GREGORIO REGINO

Because they are the papers of the judge
It is the Book of your law
It is the Book of your government
Because I know how to speak with your eagle
Because the judge knows us
Because the world knows us
Because God knows us

— MARÍA SABINA

I

In the light of the candle,
in the essence of sweet basil.
In the spirit called forth by the incense,
my life's book is laid out.

Open is my thought before the judge.
The gears of time stop short.
So that Limbo may pull back a pace.
So that the sun and moon dress up
because the images take on a face.

II

What does the smoke of the incense say as it accompanies
the words that initiate their journey to the heavens.
What is the message of the maize your palms propel
that seeks for truth there in the mystery.
In what place, what path
and on what pretext does the guardian of the earth
possess my spirit.
Today reveal it, master:
before my person,
before the eyes of God,
before the witnesses.

III

You who know the sacred,
who lead us on the pathway sown with songs.
Open the sky to me, show me the world,
start me on the path to wisdom.
Let me drink from the children who spring forth,
teach me to speak and read the language of the Wise Ones,
flood me with the power of the Gods,
inscribe my name there in the Sacred Place.
I am clean, my wings are free.
Dew will cause new words to sprout,
rain will nourish wisdom.
I am star that shines beneath the stone,
sea that dances in the blue of sky,

light that travels in raw weather.
I am sun's vein, I am song.
I am dance and chant that heals.

IV

The spirit of evil lies in wait,
the song begins.
May the words arise that open up the heavens,
the prayers that cut across the profane world.
So may the candles of white light be lit
and drip envenomed blood.
It is a mortal struggle in the Sacred Place,
it is the ransom for my spirit.
For my life these fresh leaves will go forth,
these knowing words,
these colored feathers,
these songs for this initiation.

V

Here my basil is at daybreak,
clean like the horizon:
my medicine is fresh,
my medicine is white.

In its leaves the gentle word
that opens up the heavens:
the word that gives us peace,
the word that gives us breath.

My basil will arrive where sins are purged,
will fly off clean to where dawn grows bright.
My pleas will reach into the book of records,
will free my soul from poisons that can kill me.

VI

My incense will reach the place
where it communes with life.
It will reach the house of those
who are the guardians of the earth.
It will be heard out in the place of images,
will plead its case there in the bosom of the night.

However many mouths they have,
however many tongues they may possess,
those who have knowledge of the heavens,
those conversing with the codices
and speaking with the Gods.

VII

Here is my spirit,
my oak, my cedar.
Here in my heart the prayer is born,
is with it in its journey to the heavens.

From the house of purity,
the table of the dawn.
I am asking for strength.
I am seeking justice.

The sacred book will open,
the darkness will grow bright.
In the house of writings.
In the house of the stelae.

VIII

Down to the soles of my feet.
Down to the palms of my hands.
At the apex of my thought.
At the core of my extremities.

My spirit has feet,
my soul has hands,
my veins leave tracks,
pulses of time and the way.

I can talk with the dawn,
submerge myself in turbid waters of torrential rivers,
barefoot can walk up the incline,
can hurl my song against the wind.

IX

I arrive with God the Father, God the Mother,
I have crossed seven winds,
seven levels of the heavens.
I have defied seven faces of the World Below.

Because I have eyes for looking at the night,
light enough to plumb the mystery.
Because I am a messenger who guarantees his word,
a singer who can track the soul.

In the house of purity
I come to put my calling to the test,
come to awaken secrets.
I come to seek the word,
the fresh path and the clean path.

I am a bird that prophesies the sacred,
morning star that opens the horizon,
cicada that whispers to the moon,
mist that cures the mountain.

X

Here the fiesta ends,
the road is closed, the song is over.
Lucidity is lingering in the copal,
kernels of corn close up their pages,
standing guard over the journey's secrets.

A mystery is disappearing,
new ways emerging, ways to fathom life.
The birds trace paths, the earth is fasting.
The moon confides her troubles to the sun
and dawn shakes loose on the horizon.

Here the fiesta ends,
the song rests in the morning's arms.
The children who spring forth open the world's heart,
nature is sending signals.

Translation from Spanish by Jerome Rothenberg

SELECTED BIBLIOGRAPHY

*The sources below cover the original publications of material in
this volume, along with references that may give further insights
into the life and works of María Sabina. The citations at the end of
Henry Munn's essay (page 162) can act as an additional supplement.*

PRIMARY SOURCES

Estrada, Álvaro. *Vida de María Sabina: La sabia de los hongos.* Mexico: Siglo XXI
Editores, 1977.

Estrada, Álvaro, Henry Munn, et al. *María Sabina: Her Life and Chants.* Santa
Barbara, Calif.: Ross-Erikson Publishers, 1981.

Regino, Juan Gregorio. Netzahualcóyotl Prize Address ("The poet speaks, the
mountain sings"). In *La palabra florida,* año 1, número 2, (1997).

———. *Ngata'ara stsee (Que siga lloviendo).* Mexico: Escritores en Lenguas In-
dígenas, A.C., 1999.

Rothenberg, Jerome. *New Selected Poems, 1970–1985.* New York: New Direc-
tions, 1986.

Waldman, Anne. *Fast Speaking Woman.* Pocket Poets Series, no. 33. San Fran-
cisco: City Lights Books, 1996.

Wasson, R. Gordon, et al. *María Sabina and Her Mazatec Mushroom Velada.*
New York and London: Harcourt Brace Jovanovich, 1974.

Wasson, Valentina Pavlovna, and R. Gordon Wasson. *Mushrooms, Russia, and
History.* Vol. 2. New York: Pantheon Books, 1957.

Works by Henry Munn and Homero Aridjis are previously unpublished, as is Álvaro Estrada's addendum to his "Introduction to *The Life of María Sabina.*"

ADDITIONAL WORKS ON MARÍA SABINA

Benítez, Fernando. *Los hongos alucinantes.* Mexico: Ediciones Era, 1964, 1970.

Cela, Camilo José. *María Sabina y el carro de heno, o el inventor de la guillotina.* Madrid: Biblioteca Jucar, 1974.

Fernández, Fernando, ed. "Tras la huella de María Sabina" (with articles by Álvaro Estrada, Homero Aridjis, Juan García Carrera, Nicolás Echevarría, and Fernando Fernández). *Viceversa,* no. 63 (August 1998).

Munn, Henry. "The Mushrooms of Language." In *Hallucinogens and Shamanism,* edited by Michael Harner. New York: Oxford University Press, 1973.

———. "Writing in the Imagination of an Oral Poet." In *Symposium of the Whole: A Range of Discourse Toward an Ethnopoetics,* edited by Jerome and Diane Rothenberg. Berkeley and Los Angeles: University of California Press, 1983.

DISCOGRAPHY

Mushroom Ceremony of the Mazatec Indians of Mexico. Recorded by V. P. and R. G. Wasson at Huautla de Jiménez. New York: Folkways Records, 1957.

SOURCE NOTES AND ACKNOWLEDGMENTS

Unless otherwise indicated, all works cited are by María Sabina.

THE LIFE

The Life (*La Vida*), written with Álvaro Estrada, was published in Spanish as *Vida de María Sabina: La sabia de los hongos* (Mexico: Siglo XXI Editores, 1977). The English translation first appeared in *María Sabina: Her Life and Chants,* by Álvaro Estrada, Henry Munn, et al. (Santa Barbara, Calif.: Ross-Erikson, 1981). Reprinted courtesy Álvaro Estrada. Translation reprinted courtesy Henry Munn.

THE CHANTS

"The Folkways Chant" was recorded in July 1956, and the recording was published as *Mushroom Ceremony of the Mazatec Indians of Mexico* (Folkways Records and Service Corporation, New York City, U.S.A. FR 8975). Translation from Mazatec into Spanish (1977) by Álvaro Estrada. The English version by Henry Munn is based on that translation and on the independent translation by Eloina Estrada de González. It also draws directly on the recording with the assistance of Nati Estrada. Translation reprinted courtesy Henry Munn.

"The 1970 Session: Three Excerpts" were recorded by Celerino Cerqueda and translated from Mazatec into Spanish by Eloina Estrada de González. The English version by Henry Munn is printed courtesy Henry Munn.

"The Mushroom Velada: Three Excerpts" were translated into Spanish and English by George M. and Florence H. Cowan, and appeared in Wasson's *María*

Sabina and Her Mazatec Mushroom Velada (New York and London: Harcourt Brace Jovanovich, 1974). Excerpts from *María Sabina and Her Mazatec Mushroom Velada,* © 1974 by R. Gordon Wasson, reprinted by permission of Harcourt, Inc.

COMMENTARIES & DERIVATIONS

"Introduction to *The Life of María Sabina*" was written by Álvaro Estrada and was first published in Spanish in *Vida de María Sabina: La sabia de los hongos* (Mexico: Siglo XXI Editores, 1977). The English translation by Henry Munn first appeared in *María Sabina: Her Life and Chants,* by Álvaro Estrada, Henry Munn, et al. (Santa Barbara, Calif.: Ross-Erikson, 1981). Reprinted courtesy Álvaro Estrada. Translation reprinted courtesy Henry Munn.

"Teo-Nanácatl: The Mushroom *Agape*" by Valentina Pavlovna Wasson and R. Gordon Wasson originally appeared in *Mushrooms, Russia, and History,* vol. 2 (New York: Pantheon, 1957). Reprinted courtesy Masha Britten.

"The Uniqueness of María Sabina" by Henry Munn is printed courtesy Henry Munn.

"María Sabina in Mexico City" by Homero Aridjis is printed courtesy Homero Aridjis.

Fast Speaking Woman and "Fast Speaking Woman & the Dakini Principle" by Anne Waldman originally appeared in *Fast Speaking Woman* (San Francisco: City Lights, 1975, 1996). Reprinted in a revised version courtesy Anne Waldman.

"The Little Saint of Huautla" by Jerome Rothenberg originally appeared in *New Selected Poems, 1970–1985* (New York: New Directions, 1986). Reprinted courtesy New Directions.

"The Poet Speaks, the Mountain Sings" by Juan Gregorio Regino originally appeared in *La palabra florida,* año 1, número 2 (1997). "The Song Begins" by Juan Gregorio Regino originally appeared in Mazatec and Spanish versions in *Ngata'ara stsee (Que siga lloviendo)* (Mexico: Escritores en Lenguas Indígenas, 1999). Reprinted courtesy Juan Gregorio Regino.

COPYEDITING: MELODY LACINA AT WILSTED & TAYLOR
PUBLISHING SERVICES

DESIGN AND COMPOSITION: JEFF CLARK AT WILSTED & TAYLOR
PUBLISHING SERVICES

TEXT: GRANJON

DISPLAY: AKZIDENZ GROTESQUE

PRINTER AND BINDER: THOMSON-SHORE, INC.

Printed in Great Britain
by Amazon